THE INVISIBLE GAME

ADDITIONAL PRAISE FOR *THE INVISIBLE GAME*

"Practical science at its best! *The Invisible Game* gives readers the tools and confidence to close more deals and close them faster."

—Paul J. Zak, Author of Immersion:
The Science of the Extraordinary and the Source of Happiness.

"Kai is *the* international pioneer for integrating neuroscience and psychology to meet the challenges of finding the right price. In this new milestone, together with Gaby Rehbock, he brings together all the great truths of pricing in one place."

—John Kutcher, CPP, Global Price Setting Leader, GE HealthCare

"A true [visible] game changer. *The Invisible Game* is a remarkable addition to your arsenal of books unpacking the secrets of the consumer minds and ways to increase sales. Gaby and Kai take us on a wondrous journey through behavioral economics, decision science, marketing, and sales in a very accessible, practical, and playful way. A fun read, full of interesting stories and examples that empower the readers to embark on a learning journey."

—Moran Cerf, Professor of Neuroscience and Business,
Northwestern University

"The must-read to understand relevant profit levers for all kinds of business relationships. *The Invisible Game* is written for anyone in a client-facing job, from independent contractors to managers (not only but also) working in complex retail sales and service structures."

—Rahil Ansari, CEO & Chairman Volkswagen Group Taiwan

"Highly recommended. The professional sale is an exceedingly complex game. The authors provide numerous refined moves for winning. Their insights are based on solid scientific data yet have tremendous practical impact."

—Ryan Knauss, Vice President, Monetization, VMware

THE INVISIBLE GAME

THE SECRETS AND THE SCIENCE OF
WINNING MINDS AND WINNING DEALS

KAI-MARKUS MUELLER
GABRIELE REHBOCK

WILEY

Registered Offices
John Wiley & Sons, Inc., 111 River Street, Hoboken, NJ 07030, USA
John Wiley & Sons Ltd, The Atrium, Southern Gate, Chichester, West Sussex, PO198SQ, UK

Editorial Office
The Atrium, Southern Gate, Chichester, West Sussex, PO198SQ, UK

For details of our global editorial offices, customer services, and more information about Wiley products visit us at www.wiley.com.

Wiley also publishes its books in a variety of electronic formats and by print-on-demand. Some content that appears in standard print versions of this book may not be available in other formats.

Library of Congress Cataloging-in-Publication Data Is Available:

ISBN 9781394152988 (Hardback)
ISBN 9781394152995 (ePDF)
ISBN 9781394153008 (ePub)

Cover Design: Wiley
Cover Image: © Kwangmoozaa/Getty Images

Set in 10/14.5pt ITC Franklin Gothic Std by Straive, Chennai, India
Printed and bound by CPI Group (UK) Ltd, Croydon, CRO 4YY

C9781394152988_201022

To everyone whom we have had the privilege to work with throughout our careers

CONTENTS

THE INVISIBLE GAME

INTRODUCTION: IT'S NEVER BEEN HARDER TO BE A SALESPERSON

'Jim, I have no clue why we lost this business.'

I heard that sentence come from a couple of rows in front of me on a flight from New York to Frankfurt. I smiled and respectfully tried to ignore the conversation. But the salesperson had one of those game-show-host voices that are impossible to ignore. When he continued to talk, I could hardly believe my ears.[1]

'It was some newcomer', the salesperson said, adjusting one of his earbuds. 'Basically, the same product, but they got a higher price?!? I mean, explain that one to me, huh.'

He paused for a moment when the flight attendant handed him a drink. The fact that the flight attendant called him 'Mr. Anderson' clued me in that this wasn't his first flight back from a sales negotiation.

'I followed the request by the book', Anderson said. 'No idea how this could happen. I really did not see this coming.'

Needless to say, I could empathize. After over two decades spent at negotiating tables around the world, I could recall several lost negotiations that I couldn't immediately understand or explain. But at that moment, as I watched other passengers boarding the plane, I felt a mixture of happiness and relief. Why? I was on my way back from closing an important deal,

Figure I.1 Gaby breaks down a victory in the Invisible Game

one which my team stood little chance of winning – at least on paper – against the incumbent, a multinational conglomerate.

Then Anderson's voice once again rose above the noise of baggage compartments slamming shut and seatbelts clicking.

'Yeah, yeah. You're probably right', Anderson said. 'Aurelio just wanted a change. Nothing we could have done to prevent that happening.'

Hearing the name 'Aurelio' gave me a strange chill. How slim are the chances that a procurement manager named Aurelio would reject Anderson's offer on the same day that my team had agreed to a landmark deal with a procurement manager named . . . Aurelio?

It dawned on me that the gentleman two rows ahead of me was debriefing with his headquarters about a deal he had just lost to *my* team. That moment forced me to reflect on exactly how and why we convinced Aurelio's company to work with us as their supplier.

Why did we win?

Let's start with Anderson's vague blanket justification for losing the deal. They believed that their customer just wanted 'change'. That was their fatal misperception, one that my team didn't make.

In my assessment, our competitor had apparently disregarded or dismissed the nuances and intricacies of decision making. That not only means the way that professional buyers decide which supplier gets a multi-million-dollar contract it also means the way people, in general, make decisions.

I have no idea whether Anderson and his team underestimated that complexity or were unaware of it, but in the end, it didn't matter. My team overcame the odds and won a deal that superficially looked like nothing more than a battle between me-too products, one new and one familiar. Anderson and his team had done a lot of the right things and a lot of things right, but we had won by going beyond the obvious and offering a combination of reassurance, trust, and a promising future.

For example, we knew about the behaviours that derive from the endowment effect, and that's why we can confidently say that 'change' might have been the last thing that Aurelio wanted. Richard Thaler, who won the Nobel Prize in economics in 2017 for his studies of real-world human behaviour, coined the term 'endowment effect' in 1980 to describe the situation when people demand much more to give up an object than they would be willing to pay to acquire it.[2] So we knew how difficult it would be to influence any customer, never mind Aurelio, to turn away from an incumbent.

That's why my team focused on reassurance, trust, and future opportunities. Right from the start, our reassurance strategy gave the impression of low risk and low switching costs. We were new to the customer, so we focused on relationship-building to establish trust between them and our account team. Our language, our dress, and our tone all aimed to support the perception of familiarity, as 'one of them'. It worked because it was authentic. We had a lot in common with them.

Finally, we knew we had a me-too product, so we didn't try to invent some creative or clever value claims. Instead, we stressed future opportunities by presenting Aurelio with a concrete proposal for co-innovation to drive mutual growth. In terms of prices, our choice architecture gave Aurelio some appealing trade-offs. He ultimately picked a slightly higher price in return for more resilience in their supply chain, something that we felt our competitor couldn't offer with the same level of assurance.[3]

When I returned home after that flight, I called Kai, my consultant at the time, to celebrate the success and share my experience. I had met Kai during my most difficult time as an account manager. It was in the aftermath of the Great Recession. For me, that period between 2008 and 2011 marks the time when buyers focused on generating savings from their external spending. My toolbox of relationship-selling techniques, acquired and fine-tuned during my career to that point, became obsolete. What's the use of even the most sophisticated hammer when the problem is no longer a nail?

The nightmare of seeing the old ways disappear – and having no clue about what the 'new ways' would look like – led to many sleepless nights. My margins started to decline, first slowly and then rapidly. I worked under constant fear of losing business. Whenever I doubted my sales approaches and looked for alternatives, I realized that conventional sales wisdom was an empty well. It offered no responses to the newly emerging challenges.

That's when I came across Kai's first book, *NeuroPricing*, which introduced me to some intriguing concepts.[4] When we met, he quickly hooked me on the latest insights from neuroscience and behavioural economics. His guidance helped me develop a new understanding of how people behave in negotiations and how those behaviours affect the outcomes. With a trial-and-error approach, I learned to apply those insights successfully, improved my business, and restored my confidence.

Those initial successes made me want more.

Time is money . . . but not why you think it is

Eureka moments usually come from mundane or tedious events, often by accident. Mine didn't come from a mouldy Petri dish, which is how Alexander Fleming discovered penicillin.[5] Nor did I accidentally drop a mix of India rubber and sulphur onto a hot stove and 'invent' vulcanized rubber the way Charles Goodyear did.[6]

No, mine began with a mind-numbing line of questioning to a pharmaceutical industry expert, which I mercifully shorten and summarize.[7] After 10 years in academia, I had a PhD in cognitive neuroscience in my backpack and my name on several scientific studies. Then I moved to what academics call the dark side – the real world of industry. The objective of my project at the time was to help a company set the price for a new medication.

'Would you reimburse this drug at a daily rate of €1.50?' I asked the expert.

'Absolutely', she said. So I continued the line of questioning.

'Would you reimburse this drug at a daily rate of €2.00?'

'Sure.'

'Would you reimburse this drug at a daily rate of €2.50?'

There was no immediate answer. In hindsight I'm sure her hesitation was brief, but it jarred me at the time.

'Hmmm. . . €2.50? That's a tough one', she said. 'Hmmm . . . Probably not. Hmmm. . . let's say no, OK?'

Figure I.2 Kai explains the Eureka moment that helped to inspire the Invisible Game

My questionnaire still had a few more price points above €2.50. It was now obvious that she would reject those too, but protocols required me to ask her about them anyway. This was not simply to populate the rest of the cells in my Excel sheet, but to observe how she would answer the questions and what she would say.

'Would you reimburse this drug at a daily rate of €3.00?'

'Hmmm . . . that drug does have some impressive features', she said. '€3.00? Well, I already said 'no' to a price of €2.50, right? So this has to be a "no".'

'Would you reimburse this drug at a daily rate of €3.50?'

'Nope!' she said immediately.

'Would you reimburse this drug at a daily rate of . . . .'

'No way!' she said, before I could even give her the number.

Did you see the shift in the pattern of the respondent's answers? When she thought the price was too low or too high, she said 'yes' or 'no' without hesitation. But at the price points of €2.50 and €3.00, she struggled.

That sparked my curiosity. I reckoned that this significant delay offered a glimpse into her subconscious decision making. My imagination raced all the way back to my freshman year in undergraduate psychology at the University of Tübingen, where I had taken a class in mental chronometry.

Figure I.3   An experiment with three challenges

That discipline uses software to monitor people's responses to tasks, then applies mathematical and statistical models to analyse their reaction times in order to infer what the brain is doing. The idea of mental chronometry might not attract standing-room-only lecture crowds, but it intrigued me so much that I took a student job in the reaction time lab in the psychology department. To give you an idea of what we worked on, let's try an experiment with three challenges (see Figure I.3).

The odds are very high that when you answered the third challenge, you made a conscious effort to inhibit your first impulse, which is to read the word. Applying that effort – along with the switch in tasks from reading a word to identifying an attribute – leads not only to longer response times but also to more errors.[8] In general, the tougher the mental task or the harder the decision is, the longer the response time will be. In his bestseller *Thinking, Fast and Slow*, Nobel laureate Daniel Kahneman describes this as a process where the analytical 'System 2' of our mind suppresses the automatic, fast response from 'System 1'.[9]

That survey with the pharma expert was my Eureka moment: if studying response times will get you closer to the truth than studying someone's literal answers to a question, this must have valuable practical applications in marketing. Techniques borrowed from experimental psychology and brain research could help a company answer two of marketing's most perplexing and mysterious questions: how much value do customers place on a product, and how much are they really willing to pay for it?

In terms of prices, it means that the closer you get to a buyer's 'feel good' price – the highest price that still elicits a pleasant, positive response in their mind – the longer they will take either to commit to a judgment (expensive, cheap, and so on) or to make a purchase decision.

That Eureka moment provided the inspiration to dig deeper into this intersection of science and business. I left consulting and founded my own firm with the aspiration of using neurotechnology to study consumer perception of advertisements, products, and prices. Over time, my approach and the supporting algorithms and analyses I developed – known collectively as NeuroPricing™ – became a valuable market research tool used by numerous companies.[10]

When Gaby and I met, she was eager to try out more techniques to improve her sales performance. Around that time, the application of insights from behavioural economics was becoming a popular and fascinating business topic, as best-selling books (*Predictably Irrational*, *Nudge*, and *Thinking, Fast and Slow*) and a Nobel Prize (Kahneman) attest. But neither those breakthrough ideas, nor the emerging field of neuroscience, had yet become assets to the businesspeople who still form the backbone of many industries and many supply chains around the world: B2B salespeople like Gaby.

Gaby challenged me with an excellent question that soon became our shared passion: can those consumer insights – and the ever-growing body of research behind them – transfer to her world, the vast and diverse world of intercompany sales?

The answer: Yes, they can!

The Invisible Game: Where business meets neuroscience and behavioural economics

Understanding the time lag in decision making is important, but just as valuable for a salesperson is to understand the nature of the time lag. What are the buyers thinking about? What will influence their judgment?

It didn't take us long to conclude that the conventional wisdom about sales negotiations, trainings, and outcomes offered answers that were incomplete at best. Conventional wisdom and classical economics say that buyers carefully weigh sales arguments against objective data, and then calibrate their trade-offs against corporate objectives and incentives. That's how it works, right?

Then again, maybe that's not how it works.

Maybe sales negotiations are not soulless economic encounters better suited for robots and algorithms. Do buyers really do all that careful weighing and meticulous calibrating? You'd be surprised.

The more we explored that nature of professional sales negotiations, the more we realized that there is a lot more going on, not only in the buyers' minds, but in the salespeople's minds as well. Sales negotiations take place on two very different planes simultaneously, each with its own rules. We coined the terms 'Visible Game' and 'Invisible Game' to make the distinctions between those planes intuitively clear.

In the **Visible Game**, two or more parties exchange data, facts, and figures so that each can analyse different options against a set of predefined, clear-cut criteria. These comparisons lead to a decision in favour of the one that best fits the buying criteria. This is a simple and obvious **choice**. In the absence of other differentiators, price often plays a significant role as a decision criterion. This is the kind of decision process that lends itself to automation, because algorithms outperform the human brain when it comes to analysing large amounts of data.

But early in their careers, salespeople usually come to appreciate two important lessons. First, most decisions – particularly in B2B situations – do not boil down to simple choices. They aren't the kinds of choices that a company can automate. Second, they learn that loading their customer with additional data, facts, and figures does not automatically facilitate a decision.

So what happens when there is no simple choice and no obvious solution? The brain tries to evaluate all current and future aspects of a situation and makes a **judgment call**. But because the human brain is not constructed to process large data sets or to endure complexity, it reacts by trying to simplify the situation as much as possible and as quickly as possible.

A wealth of theories and models attempt to explain decisions and attitude formation. Many of these theories and models focus on two processes that work in parallel, with some authors using technical academic phrasing to distinguish between them and others using colourful metaphors. Chaiken proposed the distinction between heuristic and systematic processing, while Petty and Cacioppo explain persuasion and attitude change in their elaboration likelihood model by alluding to the central versus the peripheral route.[11] On the simpler and elegant side, Jonathan Haidt has proposed the metaphor of the elephant and the rider.[12] The most prominent model in recent years, however, is Kahneman's distinction between System 1 and System 2.[13] It has become a foundation for how people understand behavioural economics, and that's one reason why we refer to his model frequently in our book.

In addition, many experiments have demonstrated how human behaviour deviates from economic expectations. These effects, thoroughly tested and studied, serve as the scientific foundation of this book. Heuristics, biases, and fallacies – such as hyperbolic discounting, decoys, anchors, or the base-rate neglect – describe the brain's urge for simplicity, speed, and survival. The brain needs a fast response to any given external situation.

Welcome to the world of judgment calls

The word judgment already implies a high level of subjectivity, but judgment calls have a strong common denominator: a set of human behaviours more universal than many people realize.

The human brain makes judgment calls based on the consequences of evolutionary experiences and our own life experiences. 'Fight or flight' is perhaps the most widely known evolutionary judgment call. It has secured the survival of the species. Another strong universal driver is the human need to belong. As social beings, we have a deeply rooted desire to be accepted and stay within our tribe. Complementing these evolutionary experiences are our own individual life experiences, which are highly personal and shaped by our brain's perception of success or failure in past situations. Together, these behavioural experiences form the basis for the brain's judgements, which remain imperceptible to the other parties involved.

The **Invisible Game** takes place in the space where non-explicit and subliminal behaviours influence how two or more human beings interact to achieve a deal or some other business outcome or agreement. In the Invisible Game, the brains of buyers and sellers are engaged in a non-stop contest full of **split-second decisions** that neither party notices consciously, much less understands. Winning the Invisible Game is all about harnessing these under-the-radar effects to make progress toward a more valuable and profitable business relationship.

Why did we coin the new term Invisible Game instead of using the established term Behavioural Economics? In short: because the two are not the same. The Invisible Game is partly based on behavioural science, but a number of other factors sets it apart:

1. The Invisible Game takes place in the professional sales setting, commonly also subsumed under the term 'B2B sale'. As such, it is an applied strategy derived from scientific insights, not a scientific theory in itself.

2. The Invisible Game is a novel selling strategy that assimilates many established theories and decades of practical sales experience into a unique set of rules, techniques, and guidelines. It is also a metaphor for the kinds of moves salespeople can make to shift a negotiation in their favour. In that sense, it is neither a novel construct such as System 1 or System 2, nor is it an anthology of sales war stories with a common theme.

3. The Invisible Game takes psychological, neuroeconomic mechanisms that have been studied on an individual basis and applies them to real-life business interactions involving two or more players.

4. The Invisible Game takes into account that the individuals in these business interactions are subject to their own personal learning histories and in some cases to genetically determined personality differences. Players who understand these effects may and often will use them to their advantage.

5. The Invisible Game features many moves that strongly emphasize our evolutionary history and have strong ties to evolutionary psychology. Our common ancestry makes us all 'cavepeople in designer's clothes'. We all share many fundamental preferences and aversions.

6. The Invisible Game is a given, not an option. It takes place in every negotiation and every business interaction, regardless of whether the parties know it or want it.

Successfully playing the Invisible Game requires three basic skills. The first is what we call **situational awareness**, which means that the salesperson is aware of the many effects that behavioural economics, psychology, and neuroscience have on a negotiation. The second is **defence**, so that a salesperson can counter a buyer's tactics and also learn to defend themselves from their own personal biases. The third is **offence**, so that the salesperson can make active, conscious moves to influence the outcome of the Invisible Game.

In future negotiations, salespeople will have their greatest leverage in situations that require high-stakes judgment calls that a machine cannot make. But without the right knowledge, guidance, and training, they risk losing a game they are not even aware they are playing. This leaves them with an existential choice. They can continue to play the Invisible Game passively and lose, or they can play it actively and win.

For simplicity's sake, we will frequently use the term 'salesperson' throughout the book as a collective to include anyone who is selling their goods and services to another business or trying to negotiate an outcome in their favour.

All those salespeople won't hone their sound judgment by mastering the constantly evolving technologies of the Digital Age that drive the Visible Game. Instead, they need to master a set of fundamental and innately human forces – expressed in the Invisible Game – that have hardly evolved at all since the last Ice Age. Each party in a sales negotiation is essentially a caveperson, subject to the same strong influences no matter how fancy their designer suits, how sophisticated their electronic gadgetry, or how much number-crunching they arm themselves with. These stable forces will become a source of power for salespeople once they learn how to harness them.

Learning to play the Invisible Game

The **Invisible Game** has three parts, with each one building on the insights from the previous one.

Part I: Building your situational awareness

Part I makes salespeople keenly aware of the subliminal Invisible Game, which takes place non-stop in any negotiation. By the time every sales encounter ends – whether it is a brief Zoom call, an email exchange, or a lengthy face-to-face meeting – a salesperson will have absorbed hundreds or even thousands of impressions from others and probably made just as many of impressions on them.

However, few people could recount that information explicitly, because the effects are usually pre-conscious. Part I lays the initial groundwork to help salespeople use situational awareness to understand these impressions, the effects they can have, and how to adjust their behaviour. It introduces a small number of central concepts from behavioural economics, psychology, and neuroscience and shows that salespeople can apply them with rigor and precision. The key factor is the salesperson's mindset, in the most literal sense of the word.

Part II: Playing defence and the power of 'no'

Why are prices such a touchy subject in almost every negotiation? It's not because salespeople don't 'get the maths'. It's because few people – salespeople included – realize that prices represent far more than an amount of money. They feed on context and trigger intense sensory and emotional experiences in both buyers and sellers. This applies universally, whether you are buying or selling a cup of coffee, a glass of wine, a truckload of industrial goods, or an entire manufacturing plant.

Part II shows why salespeople struggle with prices – and discounts in particular – and how they can reset their minds to overcome their internal barriers to success. Anyone with sales in their job description can take specific steps to change themselves from the inside out. They can overcome ingrained habits, respond quickly and confidently in stressful situations, and establish the rules for a negotiation rather than follow them. They can literally reset their minds so that they can recognize and play the Invisible Game with confidence.

Part III: Playing offence and the powers of influence

When a salesperson needs to adjust or increase prices, success usually depends more on influence than maths. The strength of their influence, in turn, depends on how well they have established a home-field advantage. To do that, a salesperson needs to explore the balance of power in each negotiation, then create a choice architecture that is advantageous to them by understanding the behavioural psychology and neuroscientific forces at work in the minds of buyers.

There are literally hundreds of ways for sellers to wield their influence. *The Invisible Game* curates that long list and in Part III presents the ideas and techniques that are backed by the strongest combination of solid science, practical real-world experience, and strategic relevance.

Two more things before you get started

Before you dive into Part I, we'd like to explain some of the techniques we will use to make our ideas and recommendations more accessible, and then ask you to complete one task based on your own selling experience.

As with any new skill, your ability to play and win the Invisible Game will depend on practice, recovery, and reinforcement. That's why our book includes several elements that will guide you through that process.

- **Timeouts and fun quizzes:** We will cover a lot of new ground in the book, and some sections will be more intense than others. That's why we will give you breathers so that you can step away, digest the information, and reset. Sometimes they will be pure timeouts, while on other occasions we will use a fun quiz to ease you into a new section.

- **Situations:** *The Invisible Game* includes various practical situations that help you to see how the key ideas and the underlying science work when applied to real-life selling situations that most salespeople have encountered at least once.
- **'Sticky' notes:** We will condense some of the most important ideas in the book onto notes to reinforce them and make them more memorable. You will find nine notes spread throughout the book. Of course, if there is another idea that you feel needs more reinforcement, we encourage you make your own notes as you read through the book.

Now let's get to the task based on your own experiences. Think back to Gaby's recollections of Mr. Anderson's debrief. We'd like you to do a similar debrief. If you are a professional corporate salesperson, we suggest that you think about a couple of deals you have recently participated in. Take out a piece of paper and write down the reasons why you won or lost, and note what you would do differently if you could repeat the negotiation. If you are either new to sales, or if selling is only one part of your work as a business owner or a professional, we suggest that you write down some questions you have or some aspects of sales that you find particularly frustrating.

Use that piece of paper as your bookmark, because we will refer to it from time to time to see how your answers change.

Part I

Building Your Situational Awareness

E very dedicated sports fan can name a referee's decision that did not go their way. In some cases, they will insist that even the best high-resolution, slow-motion video evidence was not definitive. So how do professional referees succeed in making high-pressure judgment calls with reasonable accuracy? After all, the pressure on them to 'get it right' in the moment is immense.

Bill Belichick, who has won a record six Super Bowls as head coach of the NFL's New England Patriots, once praised the officials' decision-making skills: 'There's no doubt those guys – all of the officials – they have such a hard job to do. I know we look at the replays and analyse them millisecond by millisecond and everybody has all of the answers on what it should be and what it shouldn't be. These guys are out there trying to do it live and at full speed. They make so many amazingly good calls and some of the plays are just so close that it's less than an inch or . . . not even a split-second.'[1]

What applies to American football also applies to soccer, the sport also more commonly known as football. Let's go back to an event that caused an international controversy in June 2004. The scene was the quarter-finals of the European Championship. With one minute left in regulation, soccer powerhouses England and Portugal stood deadlocked at 1–1 in a tense, winner-take-all match in Lisbon. Urs Meier, a world-class referee from Switzerland, awarded England a free kick in Portuguese territory.

True to his legendary reputation, David Beckham bent the ball into the box, and within the blink of an eye, England's Sol Campbell put the ball in the back of the net.[2] This last-minute goal gave England a stunning 2–1 victory and sent them to the semi-finals.

Or did it?

What transpired on that play is situational awareness at its finest. Meier needed to make a decision in the heat of the moment. Compounding that pressure were the deafening sounds of tens of thousands of screaming fans in the stadium, the invisible eyes of countless millions more watching on television, and perhaps even the excruciating never-ending scrutiny of history.[3]

He blew his whistle: No goal! He indicated that England had committed a foul and awarded Portugal a free kick.

Within a matter of hours, that fateful decision earned Meier the reputation as 'the most vilified man in football'.[4] He reportedly received 16,000 hate emails, 5,000 abusive phone calls, and even death threats. The UK retail chain Asda seemed somewhat sympathetic, but in a sarcastic way. It supposedly offered all Swiss nationals a free eye exam at one of its 68 optical centres.[5]

To this day Meier not only stands by that decision, but also by the process that led to it. What is even more amazing – until you understand his explanation – is that Meier *never even saw the foul* that led him to nullify the goal!

As he described in his book *DU Bist Die Entscheidung* [English: YOU Are the Decision],[6] Meier sensed something was odd the moment the ball went into the net. He claimed that his gut and his entire body gave him the signal, triggered by a small inconsistency that fans sitting in the stadium or watching on TV probably would never have noticed. Meier observed that England forward John Terry did not behave the way one would expect in the immediate aftermath of such an important goal. Instead of looking at his teammates to celebrate, Terry looked directly at Meier. That one instant of eye contact told the experienced referee all he needed to know. Terry had committed a foul. It turns out that he had hindered the Portuguese goalkeeper. Video replay ultimately showed that Meier's 'blind' intuitive call was indeed correct.

Meier's example from the 2004 England–Portugal match is an inspiring and instructive example of situational awareness: detecting slight deviations between a person's behaviour and what the rest of a scene presupposes that we should see instead. Meier pre-consciously knew what to look for without any interference, forethought, or second-guessing from his conscious mind. When he is confronted with ambiguous or unclear situations, Meier bases his decisions on that kind of intuition, which is now a best practice among many professional sports officials.

Making such intuitive snap judgments correctly is an important part of playing the Invisible Game successfully. The parties in sales negotiations often face similar situations, but there are some major differences between a sales negotiation and other high-pressure events such as championship sports, and not all of them work to a salesperson's advantage.

First, in a negotiation, you don't have the luxury of freezing the action to go to a more objective source, such as video replay, then spend a couple of minutes trying to understand whether you made the right decision. Rarely do you have the chance for a 'do over' if you see that you have made mistake or a misjudgment.

The second major difference is that referees are supposed to be neutral. Their decisions could go in favour of either party, ostensibly without bias. In business negotiations, there is no third party to catch infractions by the other side. You are one of the players and have to work on your own to steer the outcome in your favour.

The third difference is how the implicit 'rules of the game' have evolved, particularly the level of uncertainty around what rules to enforce. When Meier walked onto the pitch during his long career, he didn't have any idea what would transpire, but he did have some well-established constants to work with. The most basic rules of soccer are fixed and clear. At the start of the match, there were always 11 active players per side, fighting over one ball. The length and width of the field may vary from stadium to stadium, but the goals, the penalty areas, and the goal boxes always had the same strict and familiar dimensions. If only the same kinds of fixed and clear rules applied to the playing field and the teams in a sales negotiation!

These three important differences – no pause button, no impartial referee, and no fixed rules – leave many questions unanswered. What can salespeople latch onto for reliable orientation in order to gain and maintain leverage in their negotiations under uncertain and volatile conditions? Where can they find a source of stability or some semblance of consistency? Beyond that, there are important questions about the intuitive processes that Meier and others rely on when they make snap judgments or split-second decisions. What really drives this intuition? Furthermore, as a salesperson, how can you learn to harness those same forces to elevate your selling performance from good to excellent, make it stick, and make excellent performance second nature?

Chapter 1

The Forces Behind
the Invisible Game

A professor at the University of Växjö asked over 200 managers at Swedish companies how they make decisions. A small majority of managers claimed they relied on their hunches, with 32% saying they decided intuitively and 19% according to their feelings. Some 26% said they decided situationally with a 'focus on detail', and 23% said their decisions were analytically driven.[1]

These results are intriguing, because they mask a fact that helped inspire us to write this book. We are all players in the Invisible Game without necessarily being aware of the response patterns hard-wired into our brains. How actively and how well we play the Invisible Game, however, is a much different story. We cannot opt out, but at the same time, we are not powerless. Far from it! Starting with the building blocks of situational awareness, we will codify the behaviours deeply ingrained in each of us and show you how to use them to your advantage.

The foundation of situational awareness rests on a small number of vitally important behavioural, psychological, and neuroscientific concepts that every salesperson needs to master: the concept of System 1 and System 2 thinking, the concept of relativity, and the concept of anchoring. Understanding and building on these concepts is your first step to develop your own new success model for your negotiations and their outcomes.

System 1 and System 2: Partners, not rivals

Before we get to specific selling situations, we need to take a step back and understand how our brains operate. Our brains have evolved to protect us, guide us, and help us solve problems in adversarial situations.

The starting point is the way that Kahneman distinguishes between fast thinking and slow thinking: 'I describe mental life by the metaphor of two agents, called System 1 and System 2, which respectively produce fast and slow thinking.'[2]

System 2

As twenty-first-century professionals, we all recognize and value Kahneman's System 2 thinking. It is the collective term for how our mind processes data, picks the numbers, juggles and cross-checks them, and then assesses all of the 'on-paper' stuff: the economic and financial impact of proposals and counterproposals. System 2 serves as our sophisticated problem solver in the Visible Game. It produces good results in complex situations that require analysis and broader, more creative, thinking. You rely on System 2 if you are looking for an innovative idea, for a way to see connections between seemingly disparate things, or for an 'out-of-the-box' answer. System 2 works well with open-ended questions, where the answers can be surprising or ambiguous, or become better with time and critical thinking.

System 2 is what guides salespeople as they ponder, draft, rewrite, and edit a lengthy proposal or response. System 2 also has an on–off switch. Disengaging System 2 is what the Americans called 'vegging' or what the Dutch have started to call 'niksen', the art of doing absolutely nothing with the goal of recharging. This disengagement is important, because System 2 exhausts itself quickly and needs to recharge frequently. It explains why creative teams need frequent breaks or changes of scenery in order to bring in new stimulation or allow thoughts to develop further.

Situation 1.1 provides a look at our first real-life situation, one familiar to anyone who has sat in a conference room during a presentation.

Situation 1.1: Time out! Their eyes are glazing over

As the bright sun warmed up in the crowded conference room, you could feel the energy rapidly disappear. The clock seemed frozen at 1:45 pm. You clicked to another slide, your 37th in this deck, and then blanked out for a moment. What was your point again? You weren't sure anymore, and if you had asked the audience, most would also have been just as clueless. The in-person attendees sat as if they were in suspended animation. The folks on the Zoom call did their best to stay on camera and look attentive. You didn't have the next 'bio break' scheduled for another 45 minutes, because lunch wasn't too long ago. What's going on?

We have all been in these situations during very dense PowerPoint presentations. We all tend to exhaust our audience with too much information, too many words, and too many slides. When people reach a saturation point for information, they become restless, upset, tense, and tired.

What is the science behind this? System 2's effectiveness and attention span erode quickly. It is hard to digest information properly on the fly, especially after the amount of information we have received has exceeded our saturation point. Your brain needs the time to absorb and process information, resettle emotions, locate potential misinterpretations, and avoid overreactions. To accomplish that, you need an opportunity to step back and interact with others, to paraphrase what you have heard, review your notes, and maybe ask yourself some challenging questions.

What is our recommendation? The brain – not the bladder – should be the biological driver of when you need breaks and how long they should last. Timeouts should not only be frequent, but also purposeful so that people can absorb and process what they have heard so far. Prepare yourself to see people's attention take a first dip after 15 to 20 minutes.

We advise taking a break every 45 to 60 minutes. In our own experience, we know how challenging it can be to adopt such a best practice, especially if you are expected to squeeze two days of content into one day. At some point, people need real timeouts with a change of pace, scenery, or format. Working sessions are for information hunting and gathering, but you need breaks to digest all that mental food and stay on track.

We also consider timeouts to be very valuable tactical manoeuvres in any complex business negotiation for the same reasons that they are valuable in team sports. They allow a team to re-group when things start to get out of hand. We recommend agreeing in advance with your customer party on timeout opportunities that allows each party to withdraw to separate conference rooms or even a dedicated WhatsApp chat. The intent is for your group to have pre-planned opportunities to realign or simply to allow everyone's mental systems to re-calibrate.

But System 2 is not the set of thought processes in our brains that enable professional referees – or anyone else – to make split-second, high-stakes decisions with confidence. That primary thought process is known as System 1.

System 1

The idea behind System 1 is that humans have a separate mode of operation that works automatically and comprises the primal mental functions of our minds.

From an evolutionary standpoint, the responses generated by System 1 are potent and effective. Otherwise, humans would have become extinct eons ago. So much of what we think and do – or don't do – runs on autopilot. Have you ever shown up somewhere by car, but you can't remember much of the drive at all? Have you seen an empty bag of crisps or cookies, but you cannot recall finishing it? Those are just two of a nearly infinite number of ways that System 1 keeps us going and keeps us safe. It is an enormous evolutionary strength that allows us to do many things at one time.

These functions are hard-wired into our brains to such an extent that every sales negotiation takes place between cavepeople at some pre-conscious or subconscious level. No matter how much we try to disguise or suppress these primal mental functions, they will inevitably exert their influence.

System 1 produces quick decisions with good results in business-as-usual situations. It helps us to respond in situations that tend to be infor-mation poor. System 1 responds well to closed questions, such as yes/no questions or simple multiple choice.

Think of social media usage as a helpful illustration. System 1 is what leads us to immediately tap an emoji to like or dislike a post. In contrast to System 2, however, System 1 does not have an on–off switch. It only has a dimmer switch. It is not only frighteningly fast, but also *always* on. You can't pause the Invisible Game or decide not to play. There is no air-plane mode.

The journey to better sales performance is not about feeding System 2 – neither yours nor your audience's – an overwhelming amount of data and information. If the discussion devolves into two teams trying to outdo each other in terms of System 2, then the negotiation has stalled. If System 2 alone could resolve a negotiation, we would no longer need salespeople and could turn the entire sales department over to artificial intelligence (AI) and algorithms. What accelerates and enhances the journey to better sales performance is the addition of contextual

references that feed, sharpen, and improve the instant judgment provided by System 1.

The risks and benefits of System 1 thinking

The evolution of System 1 has made us very efficient and effective in many
ways, but it comes at a cost. It assumes a certain level of environmental
consistency and stability that is often not truly there. If we aren't careful,
others can capitalize on those illusions and the speed of System 1's
responses. The upside is that System 1 is an equalizer. The more we
understand that we are much more similar than we think, the more we can
learn how to use System 1 to our own advantage. Instead of fighting
hunches and signals, you facilitate them and learn to trust them because
you have expanded your knowledge base, the well of accomplishments and
experiences that System 1 draws on. This is comparable to the way we
train System 2 through traditional educational approaches.

Another characteristic of System 1 is that it has neither the ability nor
the time to construct a lie. No matter how finely tuned someone's System
2 is, it cannot prevent System 1 from reacting authentically to any given
situation in the blink of an eye. We often draw the comparison between the
race car and the snail. For almost any question, the race car (System 1)
gets to the finish line labelled 'answer' long before System 2 even gets a
chance to react.

What does this mean for the salesperson? It means that any instant
reaction from a negotiation partner has a high chance of being authentic.
The more attuned and attentive someone is to observe these reactions,
the more likely they are to detect unequivocal clues that would otherwise
be hidden in micro-expressions, micro-behaviours, or a seemingly innocuous Freudian slip.

Once your situational awareness starts to reveal these subtle System 1
signals, you will be surprised how obvious they can be and how often they

appear. Gaby has experienced situations in which her negotiation partner said 'I really like your offer' while noticeably shaking his head at the same time. The purchaser was apparently oblivious to his 'no' gesture, but Gaby wasn't. It compelled her to check on her team's position and, indeed, she found out that a competitor of hers had just submitted a new offer that the buyer found attractive. By recognizing and then acting on the 'no' gesture, Gaby and her team modified their approach and ultimately outmanoeuvred the other bidder.

Here is a simple exercise to allow you to practise recognizing these gestures and improve your own situational awareness. The next time you receive a verbal compliment – someone likes your product, your suit, or your pet – try to make a conscious effort to observe what the person's head does. Even the slightest nod confirms the compliment. Once you start making these types of observations, you will be surprised how often a positive message is accompanied by a 'no' gesture, a headshake, which means there is a conflict between words (System 2) and what the person really feels (System 1). The gesture does not always mean the person is outright lying to you. There are no such rigid, black-and-white interpretations. There are also cultural differences to take into account. In India, for example, the headshake may have several different meanings depending on its form or context.

But we can say with confidence that the gesture in Western cultures does indicate that something is off. If you are in a sales negotiation, it means that you should not take praise at face value or assume success. Your System 1 is warning you to step back and find out what is causing the discrepancy between what you heard and what you saw.

To test this and get more practice in a no-pressure environment, keep an eye out for how actors and actresses deliver the line 'I love you' in a movie or a TV show. When things build up to that romantic moment when one character confesses to have fallen in love with the other person, watch how the person's head moves when they utter the words. Often you will

notice that they will shake their head slightly, for a fraction of a second. Even Academy Award winning actors can't avoid that tell. The culprit is System 1, which cannot suppress the fact that the words and the emotions are artificial.

Recognizing the power of System 1

The conventional wisdom views the dichotomy between System 1 and System 2 as a battle between the irrational and the rational. That makes sense from the perspective of the cultured twenty-first-century professional, who would rather view the 'animal' side through the 'civilized' lens rather than vice versa. However, that perspective is flawed, because it evaluates

System 1 through the lens of System 2. In our view, *both* sides are rational in their own contexts. Both make intrinsic sense, and neither should be subordinated to the other. Both therefore need to be understood on their own terms and placed on equal footing when you are in a negotiation.

We believe that the autopilot of System 1 is not only undervalued, but massively undertrained. There are huge differences in the quality and reliability of a person's autopilot. It is not an 'either you have it or you don't' thing. The better your pre-programming is, the better your System 1 autopilot will perform. But most salespeople don't focus on pre-programming and refining this function. They don't realize how important it is to manage the experiences, accomplishments, and flows of information that fuel and fine-tune their autopilot.

Getting System 1 the attention it deserves is often an uphill battle. Witness how companies construct and conduct their sales trainings, which tend to emphasize System 2 and gloss over System 1. Companies err on the side of more facts, more data, and more hard analyses because data is the coin of the realm in today's digital age. This bias in favour of System 2 also manifests itself in the labels 'hard' and 'soft' skills, a distinction that belittles System 1. The fact that supposedly 'soft' skills defy easy quantification and black-and-white comparisons does not make them less powerful or more difficult to master than the hard skills that companies prize.

The food or fuel for System 2 is data and analyses. The food or fuel for System 1 is exposure and experience. Expanding System 1's knowledge base in this way is a modern expression of a primitive survival skill, from a time when automatic or intuitive behaviours meant the difference between life and death. Learning from successful experiences is a skill, even if the experiences are simulated. That's how professional athletes, musicians, and other people with superior performance gain an edge through practice.

In 2019, the Washington Nationals baseball team won the Major League Baseball World Series, and outfielder Adam Eaton had one of the most important hits in the final game. How he accomplished that feat in a stressful, high-stakes situation is not only an example of System 1 overriding System 2 at a decisive moment, but also an example of how important time commitments and repetition are to training your personal autopilot.

Eaton practices hitting a ball off a batting tee every day, rather than having someone throw him a ball. And he makes the drill as hard as possible.[3]

'High-inside tee is an uncomfortable drill, but it teaches body control', Eaton explained. 'I work on this every day.'

That hard work paid off handsomely with a contribution to a championship. In the live action of the do-or-die final game of the World Series, Eaton saw a pitch coming and told himself 'No, don't swing!' But System 1 kicked in immediately. Eaton swung the bat and got a successful hit.

'It was kind of cool to have a "blackout moment" where your body just takes over', Eaton said. 'It's a beautiful thing and you think "how did I do that?" but there was hardly any thought process.'

Without his daily training, it is doubtful that Eaton would have had his 'blackout moment' at that critical time.

Achieving this well-coordinated combination between System 1 and System 2 takes training. Like muscle or endurance training, it becomes stronger and more effective the more frequently it is practised and honed.

Extending the analogy from sports to sales, we recommend you constantly push the boundaries of your own knowledge base. Seek to break your habits. System 1 needs more experiences and impressions to process, so that it has a greater array of images, patterns, and feelings to rely on when it makes snap judgments. You tip the scales in your favour when you have a greater set of experiences to base your responses on.

Learning to sell with System 1 and System 2 is like being ambidextrous. Suppressing System 1 while emphasizing System 2 is like playing tennis only with your forehand and or playing basketball by dribbling only with your right hand. You become predictable and easier to defend, because the other team can overplay against you and knows that your options are limited.

In other words, a key realization for situational awareness is that the processing of a situation is not a black-and-white case of only System 1 or System 2. The reality is that many decisions involve both sides working together. Think back to situations when you and your colleagues have conducted data analyses, did some scenario planning, and decided on an option, only to have one person have the courage and forethought to speak up and say 'That just doesn't feel right.' Those reactions deserve full exploration, yet in many cases, people tend to downplay them or dismiss them entirely. Conversely, many successful System 1 responses – such as Eaton's hit in Game 7 – occur because lengthy periods of analysis preceded them before the do-or-die situation arose. System 1 and System 2 should be treated as equal partners rather than as opposing forces or in a subordinate relationship to each other.

In negotiations, we see star performers excel in both areas. Their success depends on their ability to respond quickly and confidently in highly stressful situations. It also depends on their ability to distinguish between the authentic and the insincere, between true and false, and between threats (requiring a defensive response) and opportunities (requiring an offensive response). They outperform their negotiation partners through their excellence in both System 1 and System 2 processes. They learn to tap into the strengths of both systems and train their intuitive behaviours so that their responses are intentional rather than purely reflexive. The challenge for salespeople lies in deriving the greatest combined benefits from each force so that they can win both the Invisible Game and the Visible Game.

Chapter 2

All Sales Are Won and Lost on Illusions

The one constant – the one stable and consistent aspect of sales negotiations – is that *all sales are won and lost on illusions*. Each business partner competes primarily based on what they believe about a situation. Let's be honest. Anyone's interpretation of any situation reflects a large portion of wishful thinking and illusions. Think back again to Mr. Anderson's debrief in the introduction. He went into that negotiation believing a certain set of things to be true, but his interpretation clashed with what the buyer, Aurelio, was really thinking.

Without a keen level of situational awareness and System 1 training, salespeople's reading and interpretation of a negotiating context risks being distorted by two dangerous illusions: stability and success.

The stability illusion: When the path to dinner leads to death

Cavepeople learned to follow the tracks of certain animals, because their experience and their inherited oral history kept things simple: some paths led to dinner, while other paths led to death. Their survival depended on knowing the difference.

Their twenty-first-century counterparts on sales teams view their jobs the same way. They develop strategies and sets of behaviours that they can apply over and over in the name of efficiency. But this sense of stability – and the reasoning behind it – is an illusion, especially in a business world undergoing significant transformation. The greater the degree of transformation in an industry, the more dangerous the illusion. This is how System 1 can trap a salesperson.

Salespeople who labour under the stability illusion like to think that their own business environment remains more or less stable from year to year, and that their customer's behaviour doesn't change in any meaningful way. They draw a correlation between stability and success, particularly for long-term buyer–seller relationships. But that correlation is only an artifact of their memory.

The stability illusion shows up in the expected responses to certain patterns. If salespeople say 'X' to the customer, they anticipate a certain response, and conversely, when the customer says 'Y' the salespeople tend to have a standard, almost automatic response at hand based on prior experiences and activated by System 1. Conventional sales training reinforces this behaviour by investing a considerable amount of time in sales manuals with detailed instructions that cover everything from opening a sales call to closing the deal.

Undoubtedly, learning these kinds of responses can be very helpful for salespeople in training. The responses provide them with an initial basis to programme their System 1. Having that solid initial knowledge base can alleviate their anxiety and fear. For them, this sense of stability is certainly comforting and desirable. But over time, they need to be careful that this initial knowledge base does not become their *only* knowledge base, a trap that treats apparent cause-and-effect connections as absolute givens. The dangers arise when these responses assume a fixed reality taken at face value and the salesperson stops trying to figure out what is going on under the surface. When savvy purchasers meet salespeople with well-defined routine behaviours, they will use these rigid routines against them, because they can predict the responses that certain statements will trigger.

In Situation 2.1 we look at a common situation that illustrates how strong and pervasive the stability illusion is.

Situation 2.1: Encountering the 'them' and 'this' of your firm for the first time

It is Timothy Brown's first day in his new role as a sales representative at Chicago Entrepreneurs Inc. After a short introduction to the rest of the sales team, Timothy gets assigned to Bob, one of the company's sales veterans. Bob's role is to show Tim how things are done.

Bob repeatedly peppers Tim with his advice in sentences such as 'This is what got us here', 'This is how they built this place', or 'This is how it works with our customers.' On any given day, countless sentences like Bob's echo from the walls of countless offices around the world.

Knowing the 'them' and 'this' of your firm is what makes you fast and efficient. It helps newcomers settle in. It may even help you to be a fast negotiator. At the same time, it is what makes the experienced salesperson too dependable, and worse, predictable for any professional buyer.

What is the science behind this? This is System 1's preferred way of acquiring 'survival' knowledge, a way that has evolved to transmit best practices from generation to generation. It is similar to the era when cavepeople sat at a campfire and told each other how to survive in their group and their environment. Knowing how things are done here and believing in the stability of your (customer) environment creates a nice comfort zone. However, the 'this' passed on by 'them' in the firm is precisely what makes salespeople susceptible, as their System 1 grows stale over time.

In times of transformation, it is risky for old recipes to encounter new environments. That is where the uncertainties of today's selling environments pose risks. When business environments are in transition, old answers can't solve the new equations.

> **What is our recommendation?** Without going into a drawn-out discussion of what critical thinking means and how it works, we will instead offer a technique to apply it. You should refresh and expand your trained sales responses and challenge your assumptions by asking yourself open questions. Do you know something for a fact or simply *think* you know it? Do you believe something is true or have you *actually asked* the customer in order to validate or refute it? Confronting yourself with 'What if. . .' challenges can also expand your views effectively.

Before you continue, take a brief timeout to think back to your own initiation into a company or your first conversations with a mentor. How much of their advice came with sentences like Bob's? How many times did you wonder about the advice, even if you didn't challenge it?

The success illusion: Whose game did you actually win?

Salespeople are also susceptible to the success illusion, which System 1 will reinforce if they aren't careful. How can success be an illusion? After all, the whole point of the negotiation is to win the deal on the best possible terms, right?

The success illusion occurs when salespeople feel convinced that they have achieved the best possible outcome, but in reality they did extremely well within a negotiation frame established by their opponent. Winning on the purchaser's terms is one of the big drivers behind the success illusion. In some situations, the salesperson has made a concession or a compromise to achieve success in the negotiation, but the concession or compromise was either too large or was unnecessary. The reality framed for the negotiation could have and should have been different, especially when that reality was determined by the purchaser or by the legacy of past negotiations.

The worst-case scenario is falling prey to both the stability illusion and the success illusion at the same time in the same negotiation. You walk in thinking it's the 'same old same old'. You're taking what you hear from the procurement person at face value and you're taking the numbers that they provide you with as givens. Then after the close, you walk out thinking you did the best you could under the circumstances. But who says those circumstances were the best for you in the first place? As harsh as it may sound, the perception of success was all in your head. The outcome could have been much better.

We safely assume – based on our own experiences and all the stories we have heard over the years – that every salesperson has fallen victim to at least one of these two illusions. To be more precise, it means that at one time or another, all salespeople have acted in accordance with their own intuitive hunches, impulses, and ingrained behaviours, but did so with an under-informed autopilot that hampered their situational awareness. Their autopilot may have had extensive knowledge and experience in a few narrowly defined areas, but it lacked the breadth necessary to recognize and process other patterns or events.

As we will show in the Chapters 3 and 4, the important step for salespeople is not to avoid these illusions and their potentially harmful effects. The important step is to learn to control the illusions themselves by managing the impressions they send and interpreting the ones received more critically.

Chapter 3

Controlling Illusions = Controlling the Deal

Let's take a quick pop quiz. From the list below, pick out the statement that is false:

- Shaving makes hair grow back thicker.
- Toilets flush in different directions in the Northern and Southern hemispheres.
- The forbidden fruit of Adam and Eve was an apple.
- Vikings wore horns on their helmets.
- Bulls become angry at the colour red.

It is always fascinating to watch people discuss these statements. Some people decide on their answer quickly. Others narrow the list down and then have a long debate over the two or three that remain. Over the years, we have learned that everyone who has taken this quiz has one thing in common. They are all winners, because their selection doesn't matter. All of the statements are false.

The statements demonstrate what happens when pieces of information flow through culture unchecked and unchallenged. Years, decades, or even centuries of repetition and coincidence can turn a notion into a perceived fact. That occurs in corporate cultures as well, not only in national or ethnic ones. When no one doubts a statement's veracity anymore, no one applies any effort to question it.

This is known as the illusory truth effect.[1,2] It occurs when the brain starts to accept and believe in an appealing message that is being repeated constantly over time without any contradiction or any evidence to cast serious doubt. Our minds literally take the statement for granted.

Salespeople can also use the illusory truth effect to their advantage, especially when they need to get their points across in a noisy environment (Situation 3.1).

Situation 3.1: I always come up with new ideas, but somehow, I cannot get heard

It is the classic daydream of anyone at work. We've all had it. Instead of 'Once upon a time . . .' these adventure stories begin with 'If I were in charge . . . .' You have an idea for a change. It could be a tweak to the way your value proposition is phrased. It could be the sources you use for some of your data. Or it could be something much more fundamental, such as a change to an established process in your department. The problem is that no one seems to be listening to your ideas. They might hear the words, but they aren't getting the concept and its benefits, nor are they taking you seriously.

These daydreams arise from the frustration that the processes we follow explicitly and implicitly in our business, and the hard and soft guidelines that govern those processes, are not our own. When we have a suggestion of any sort – from a small tweak to a better way to do something – we want others to hear our ideas and support us. This is an occasion when the science around System 1 calls for an offensive response, rather than a defensive response based on awareness of an effect.

What is the science behind this? This source of power in this situation is the illusory-truth effect. Research on the illusory-truth effect demonstrates that repeated statements are easier to process, and subsequently perceived to be more truthful than entirely new statements.

There is still a defensive angle, however, with respect to the illusory-truth effect. The repetition of short, compelling statements is one way that advertisers, governments, and other institutions try to instil beliefs in a particular group. In its benign form, think of all the classic advertising slogans you can recall, and the feelings you associate with them. It is a trick to mix newness with familiarity.

Our recommendation: Sales teams can use this technique to their advantage proactively, especially when they are introducing new brands or products. A new idea does not sell itself. It requires an appealing message repeated often, without change, over a longer period. It takes time for the message to settle into the buyer's or the R&D person's brain before they start to attribute some truth to it. The newer and more innovative the idea is, the more time you will need to spend on preparing the other side for acceptance.

This is one reason why very innovative ideas often fail at first. System 1 rejects them as unfeasible, outside the rules, or 'too new'. It has not had enough time to internalize them. It is vulnerable to visceral reactions, but repeated consistent messaging can calm those reactions. With sufficient time, other people may start repeating your message or co-op some of your language, which will reinforce the effect.

Selling to System 1: Do first impressions really matter?

You have probably heard the old cliché from your parents or grandparents: 'You never have a second chance to make a first impression.' As with any cliché, one has to wonder whether the truth behind it is illusory or real. What do you think?

We'll give you the answer quickly this time. Many of the clichés and stories you may have heard about sizing up another party, about giving and making a first impression, and about setting a scene are valid. They all have their ultimate roots in System 1. In short, System 1 plays a role in sales negotiations right from the outset.

Doubters often cite a lack of credible resources to explain these phenomena. The usual explanations come from a combination of inherited oral culture and personal experience. The explanation in Situation 3.2 comes from science. When we strip away cultural differences, types of industries, and other superficial differentiators, there are some fundamental human activities that take place when people meet. These constant and consistent activities are the common denominator on which a salesperson can build offensive and defensive strategies for winning the Invisible Game.

Situation 3.2: The 'bean counter' walks into your meeting

You have seen that person, straight out of Hollywood casting, walk into one of your negotiations. They dress so conservatively that they blend in with the furniture in the conference room. The most exercise they seem to get is from removing a thick binder from a high shelf. You anticipate that their voice is monotone, but it can probably rise and become emphatic when they need to protect numbers as if they were protecting their own children from a dangerous predator. A thought quickly flashes across the news ticker at the bottom of the screen in your mind's eye: 'Breaking News: This Meeting Will Be Terrible.'

Are we typecasting and stereotyping with that description? As politically incorrect and inappropriate as it might seem in writing, that is exactly what System 1 does in its biologically hard-wired efforts to help us. In the world of System 1, we carry an image of 'bean counter' in our memory, and if someone matches the picture, our minds will quickly fill in all the blanks for us about that person. Ditto for someone that looks like a librarian, a fashion model, or a hippie. It can be extremely difficult for us to articulate precisely what we think about the person, and how they might respond to our overtures, but rest assured, your System 1 has a plan.

What is the science behind this? System 1 is relying on the availability heuristic.[3] That mental shortcut relies on immediate examples that come to a person's mind when evaluating a specific topic, concept, method, person, or decision. This explains another frequent comment that we hear from sales-people, that 'in our company, the first explanation or idea is usually considered to be the best choice'. The rationale one hears to defend that statement is that your gut reaction or your 'blink' answer (to borrow a phrase from Malcolm Gladwell) has merit. It does not come from out of the blue, but rather has some solid basis.

The basis is System 1's application of the availability heuristic. It is performing an instantaneous form of pattern matching. It sifts through images, experiences, and sensations in our minds to find the closest match or to pass judgment, and it allows us to respond almost instantaneously.

Our recommendation: You should be very consciously aware of the first impression *you* leave with new contacts. The purchasers are also 'always on'. We are all human and thus all equally subject to same behavioural, psychological, and neuroscientific effects. That is one of the most compelling aspects of these forces and how they apply to negotiations.

That means that the people on the other side of the table are judging you – whether they know it or not – in the same way according to the availability heuristic. This mechanism is identical and universal. The only difference across people is the set of images, experiences, and sensations that they draw their matches from.

Clothing is one of the first and strongest triggers for a first impression. How many times have you left a meeting – no matter how serious the topic – and the first question you ask aloud is something similar to 'what was up with that awful tie?' or 'did you see those shoes?' Coco Chanel once famously said: 'Dress shabbily and they remember the dress; dress impeccably and they remember the woman.'[4] Or as designer Karl Lagerfeld said: 'Sweatpants are a sign of defeat. You lost control of your life so you bought some sweatpants.'[5]

Most importantly, the manner of dress should fit the environment. If the objective is to establish a level of trust and a potential for partnership, it can make sense to adopt the dress code of the other party. We know of one management consultant whose team wore business suits to an initial meeting with a potential customer in the entertainment industry. During a break, the leader of the potential customer pulled the consultant aside and delivered a blunt message: 'If you want to work here, lose the suits. You're scaring people. They see suits and think you are here to cut their jobs.' From that day on, the consulting team's dress code ranged from business casual to jeans.

Likewise, the choice of organizational positions sends a message about the salespeople and the company they represent. The more complex and incompatible the job titles seem, the greater the risk that the other side will either put its guard up or be dismissive. Your hot-shot 24-year-old team member may truly be the best and brightest person you have ever hired. But when the person on the other side is old enough to be that team member's parent and then sees 'executive vice president' or 'associate partner' on their business card, an immediate mistrustful or resentful reaction should not come as a surprise. System 1 says 'I do not like this.' The same thinking applies when the 'Vice President and Senior Director of Customer and Key Account Relations' meets a purchasing team in a company that has only 'purchasers' and 'senior purchasers'.

The complexity of a company's hierarchy sends a message about how the company thinks and operates. First encounters need to reduce the information asymmetry between the two parties, not confuse it or aggravate it. Your entire appearance, from your clothes to your business card, needs to fit to the message you intend to send to your customer and *not* to your position within your company.

Another important opportunity to make a first impression occurs when someone starts a new sales job. Let's assume you are succeeding someone in a given role. Planning for that new job warrants a System 2 analysis of the business, the nature of the role, the person who previously held that job, and the customers that person interacted with. We recommend that you write down the strengths and weaknesses as well as the 'natural pref-erences' of your predecessor.[6] What did they deliver that the customer considered valuable? What behaviours was the customer accustomed to? On a separate piece of paper, we suggest that you write down your own strengths and weaknesses.

Finally, ask yourself and your new boss about the overarching objective of your new assignment, beyond the numbers. Are you supposed to main-tain the business relationship 'as is' or move it in a particular direction? Are you supposed to ensure sustained success or initiate a fresh start? Will you be introducing new products or services or a new basis for the relationship? Answering those questions will help you and your manager to formulate qualitative goals.

To develop your plan for a first impression, you match your strengths – your own natural preferences – against those qualitative goals. In a 'main-tain' situation, success depends on how well you adapt to what the customer is used to from your predecessor, the one who established the existing level of trust. Then you can weave in your own ideas and play to your strengths. A fresh start, however, requires a different approach. Change must be visible and unmistakable from Day One. The strongest signals – and the easiest ones to apply – are different clothing and a dif-ferent communication style to reinforce the message of change. If you come with an agenda of change, but mimic your predecessor, you send a mixed message. Change should look and feel like change, not just sound like it.

In short: be conscious of your stereotypes and categorizations, but don't neglect the signals you are sending. Likewise, you should beware of biases due to legacy. Mastered past experiences are what System 1 matches against. You should start to mistrust feelings such as 'this is how things have to be done' or comments such as 'the way we have always done it has always worked, so it must be the best way'.

The next quiz question involves a little bit of maths. In accordance with a rule for determining the next number in a sequence, we list the following numbers: 1, 3, 5, 15, 17, 51. Can you figure out what the next number in the sequence is? We will reveal the answer after Situation 3.3.

Situation 3.3: My customer is just going through a phase . . . right?

You go into a meeting and notice right away that something is off. Your purchasing contact is acting a little strange, but you are willing to cut him some slack. They have had some organizational and leadership changes there. You and your contact have had many years of fruitful collaboration, and you attribute the weird behaviour to his need to adapt to the personality of his new boss. So your conclusion is clear: let's give them some time so that the new boss can get onboard and understand how things are done between us. After all, we can rely on a long-standing relationship with that company and we know the purchaser likes our products and likes us.

This may not look like a problem at first glance. But your conclusion in this case is clearly under the influence of System 1. Your brain has created an illusion of stability, thanks to your long-standing relationship with the customer. It wants to preserve the illusion and treats the weird behaviour of your contact as a blip or a minor aberration. You think that it is only a matter of time before everything converges back to the normal baseline that the two of you have followed for years.

What is the science behind this? In this case, System 1 is yielding to what psychologists call the confirmation bias.[7] When confronted with a change that does not appear to be an immediate or existential threat, people tend look for any information that will confirm their pre-existing beliefs. It influences how they search for, interpret, favour, and recall information. This makes it easy to confirm and reinforce the stability and success illusions.

The downside, however, is that your mind also tends to switch off the critical thinking that System 2 ought to be doing. Instead of putting up your antennae to search for more clues to explain the strange behaviours – and consider their implications for the ongoing relationship – you stifle any impulse to challenge the long-standing status quo. The underlying cause of the behavioural change might be coming from their side, or it might be on yours. This is particularly risky in times of transformation. Our minds are set up for efficiency and prefer the known to the unknown, so we have a natural tendency to resist change. We like to run on autopilot and we are in fact designed for it. You might know that same feeling from shopping if your grocery store has changed the store layout. Even when orange juice is now in aisle 5 instead of aisle 8, we may find ourselves walking on autopilot to aisle 8 a few times before we have reprogrammed ourselves.

The danger is that you could ignore problems that are on the horizon and miss clues that could allow you to act before the consequences are irreversible.

Our recommendation: System 1 and System 2 can only match against the information they have. We recommend that you deepen your understanding of the current situation and broaden your perspective. Find a devil's advocate who can provide an independent outside view that broadens your perspective. You can also be your own devil's advocate when you encounter behavioural changes. Have System 2 challenge System 1. Increase the frequency of contact with your customer and ask open questions along the lines of:

- What is the customer's bigger picture?
- What could be the new purchaser's mandate?
- How and when do they re-evaluate their suppliers?

You cannot know everything that goes on in your customer's company. But when checking up on a regular basis – especially during times of personnel changes – it is worth taking a distanced, objective look at your customer. This is not an invitation to treat every change as if it's another episode from *Only The Paranoid Survive*, the memoir by Intel's co-founder Andy Grove. At the same time, your assumptions about your customer should get a regular refresh. Otherwise, you might limit yourself and might miss some big opportunity your competition could see and pursue.

Now let's return to the maths problem. When Kai poses this challenge during one of his lectures, someone in the class will quickly and excitedly shouts out '53'.

'Correct!' Kai will say. Then he will ask what the rule is.

'The rule is +2, x3, +2, x3, and so on', the student says. Then the class falls into a bewildered silence when Kai disagrees.

'No, that is not the rule', he says. 'Try again.'

The students work out all kinds of rules that lead back to 53, and in each case, Kai says 'no' despite their protestations that he should check his arithmetic or that he is just being standoffish on purpose.

The actual rule is far simpler: each number needs to be higher than the previous one, or in mathematical terms, n>n-1. The students saw many patterns while working under the assumption – never stated by Kai – that there was one and only one answer to the question of 'what number is next?' When the students stopped trying to confirm what they thought they knew – that 53 was *the* answer – they started suggesting different answers and eventually figured out the rule. Only a method of falsification can challenge the confirmation bias, but never a method of verification.

Framing: Controlling the context

There once was a monk who asked the abbot at his monastery if he may smoke while praying. Shocked at the crudeness and utter disrespect the monk displayed, the abbot told him 'no' and ordered him immediately to go to confession.[8]

The next week, the abbot left to embark on a pilgrimage. Cigarette in hand, the same monk approached the abbot's replacement.

'May I pray while I'm smoking?' he asked.

'Of course,' the new abbot said, impressed with the monk's dedication.

What the monk did in that sequence is known as framing, an essential skill for anyone in a negotiation. Whoever sets the conditions controls how a negotiation will go. Similarly, whoever sets the logical connections, the sequence of events, and nature of the language (positive or negative tone, for example) exerts a decisive influence over the outcome of the negotiation. There are countless examples of companies that boosted the sales of a product simply by changing either the tone of the messaging or the nature of the positioning.

A real-life scenario (Situation 3.4) illustrates the power of framing.

Situation 3.4: I feel betrayed by my customer. We hit every mark and still lost the deal

You meet your customer's requests every step of the way. All through the project phase, you received tremendously positive feedback. You think you played the game perfectly. Nonetheless, when the phone call came, you could hardly believe your ears. Your competition won the business, supposedly because they introduced a new product feature. It is no surprise that you feel betrayed. You played your strongest hand well and went all-out to meet all the customer's requirements. And you still lost.

Those deals are among the most frustrating kinds of losses. You didn't see the 'no' coming. That light at the end of the tunnel turned out to be an onrushing freight train. You have no idea what you did wrong. Everything you submitted and every step you took was met with an enthusiastic response from the customer. There was apparently no signal whatsoever.

What is the science behind this? The specific term here is schema. People sometimes substitute mindset for this, but the more precise word is schema, which is 'a knowledge structure consisting of any organized body of stored information'.[9] Gaby would use this analogy: 'Think of it as an advanced form of pattern matching. If I tell you "we are going to watch the football game this afternoon at the bar", your brain will automatically call up a bunch of images of what to wear, what to talk about, what mood to expect, and what food and drink to order. That happens because "football game at a bar" is kind of a social pattern or schema with its own set of behaviours associated with it.'

Similarly, if someone says 'party', we expect people to act cheerful, excited, talkative, and maybe a little silly. If we say 'formal party', the expectations change, because schemas influence perception, attention, and behaviour.

The sales negotiation in the situation above had a particular schema that the sales team can easily and comfortably respond to and follow without challenge. If we extend this to use the term 'mindset' as well, we could say that the mindset is a person's particular frame of mind, based on the existence of a certain schema. It is how a person frames an interaction.

Our recommendation: In your preparation, you should challenge the schema of the negotiation and its parameters. This does not mean that you must confront your customer or rebel against what they have asked. It means that you should think through the frames of the negotiation – and the rationale behind each aspect – rather than accept them at face value. Remember, the customer established the frame for this negotiation and made a significant yet mostly invisible effort to influence the schema. You followed. Accepting it without question means that you are willingly playing their game.

Ask yourself what project parameters could change during the negotiation, the process, or the interaction. In a world where uncertainty is the only constant, goals and parameters can change quickly and significantly. Imagine how your competition could influence and take advantage of such changes to beat you. What are your potential blind spots, and what aspects might the customer be concealing from you? Maybe there is an implied 'above and beyond' in what the customer is asking?

One effective procedure is to conduct a 'pre-postmortem.' As depressing as that phrase may sound, it can be a powerful learning experience to pretend that you lost the deal, then ask yourself how and why that happened. What did you miss? What pieces of information could have changed the course of the negotiation?

Many outcomes come down to how well you know the buyers themselves. It is not unusual for buyers to have extensive profiles on LinkedIn, or to publish their thoughts on other professional and personal platforms. Researching them and their firm across publicly available platforms, and continually refreshing that knowledge, is not stalking. It's good business, with System 1 and System 2 working hand in hand.

Another popular example of framing is the 'monkey business' illusion. A team of people passes a basketball to each other, and the person watching the video is asked to count how many passes the team makes. The viewer's focus on counting the passes causes them to miss many other events that take place in plain sight and which are obvious in hindsight. The point is that we miss a lot when we let others determine where we should focus our attention.[10]

Quick review: Feeding System 1 and building your situational awareness

System 1 needs enough experiences and patterns to draw on so that it can inform your gut that something is correct, odd, or risky. The word 'experi-ence' does not mean a number of years, but rather the breadth and depth of situations someone has encountered. A salesperson with 20 years in their role, but little variation in situational experience may not have the range and accuracy of judgment of a colleague who has 5 or 10 years in their role, but draws on exposure to many different people, challenges, sell-ing situations, and opportunities. Even simulated experience can prove beneficial.

That underscores the importance of honing your System 1 skills, from a defensive and an offensive standpoint. The more you build up System 1 by mastering new experiences, the greater your capabilities will be to play defence and offence with confidence. You control your behaviours by mak-ing them intentional and not only intuitive.

By defence, we mean that you can trust your gut as a guide when you receive a signal during a negotiation. By offence, we mean that you can try to influence the System 1 responses of others and use them to your side's advantage in a negotiation. Either way, we recommend that you hone your split-second judgment. You train for trust in the same way as the professional referees we mentioned at the beginning of Part I. You increase your chances of triggering a positive System 1 response from a customer when you follow these guidelines for structuring and delivering information:

- Reduce complexity as much as possible, because the human brain is easily overwhelmed by too much information.
- Avoid conflicting information, because conflicts make it harder for System 1 to pattern-match and trust its judgment.
- Signal urgency with short messages.
- Provide one piece of information at a time.
- When in doubt, repeat a previous piece of information rather than provide a new one, because repetition serves as reinforcement.

Chapter 4

Relativity and Anchoring: The Illusion of Numbers

Imagine a suitcase that you have packed for a winter vacation. Maybe you have crammed it full of sweatpants, long underwear, woollen socks, and boots. Throw in a good book or two and maybe a gift for relatives, and you are ready to go! You rush out the door, get into the car, and drive off.

As you cruise down the motorway to the airport, questions inevitably pop up. Did we lock the doors? Yes. Did we adjust the thermostat? Yes. Then comes the question that has everyone in the car baffled and panicked as you think ahead to the check-in counter: how much does your suitcase weigh?

We (Gaby and Kai) occasionally conduct an experiment along those lines with one of our own personal suitcases. We ask people to guess how much the suitcase weighs, without the benefit of using a scale. The range of numbers that people come up with is endlessly fascinating. Rarely does anyone get the answer correct, and even rarer is the person who does so with confidence.

There is a biological and neuroscientific reason why nobody can reliably guess the weight of a suitcase. People have a hard time estimating weights because our brains lack internal meters for them. Humans do not think in absolute terms. We do not come equipped with natural thermometers, scales, clocks, ways to measure long distances, ways to measure value, or ways to quantify success. We are hard-wired for a qualitative world of relative relationships. The meanings we assign to numbers are illusions, because we are quantifying things that have not been quantified for most of our species' existence.

The concept at work here is called relativity. That is not relativity in the sense of Albert Einstein's famous physics theory, but rather in the sense of how our brain perceives the world for us and assesses the threats in it. It applies to weights and temperatures. That reminds us of an anecdote about how to convert a Fahrenheit temperature to one in Celsius.

'Forget all that arithmetic and formulas', an experienced fisherman once told us. 'It's really easy. If you have 50 degrees Fahrenheit, that's 10 Celsius. Then 70 degrees is 20 Celsius, and 90 degrees is 30 Celsius.'

Informed that his maths was always off by a few degrees – and got worse as the temperature rose – he smiled and responded: 'Without a thermometer, can you honestly tell me the difference between 68 and 70 degrees? Didn't think so.'

For System 1, the important thing is not the information as such, but the variation or degree of contrast between two pieces of information. Biologically speaking – for humans anyway – the difference between 68 and 70 degrees is meaningless. It is a totally artificial 'System 2' way of making sense of the world. System 1 only needs to know when it gets too warm to be comfortable, or so hot that you need to flee the fire.

Situation 4.1 looks at some aspects of negotiations where relativity exerts a strong and direct influence on the potential outcomes.

Situation 4.1: The new buyer has no experience in my industry

You are working with a new buyer that comes in fresh from an entirely differ-ent industry. He is quickly becoming a distraction at your meetings, because all of the examples he brings up are from the other industry.

Your industry is foreign to the new buyer, which means that there is no common basis for judgment. What is good or bad? What is important or unimportant? What is new or old? In the absence of those bearings, he is free to make comparisons to his previous industry and is searching for the right context that will allow him to understand your industry.

What is the science behind this? This is one form of the relativity of per-ception. Your industry is being measured and judged against a benchmark that is probably irrelevant. But the more that work goes on within the buyer's brain, the more that the comparisons he draws become firm reference points. They will be harder to dislodge as he builds his own illusions of stability. Every-one needs content and context, and the new buyer is simply searching for orientation. The true challenge is to determine the depth of information you should provide and how much you should invest in that effort.

Our recommendation: Don't let the buyer's brains create their own sets of reference points. The fact that the buyer is revealing his ignorance of your industry – intentionally or not – is an open invitation for you to provide the context for him. Seize that opportunity to set the frames. In fact, getting the new buyer onboard – with general information about your industry, your com-pany, and your operating model – is something that you should undertake and ideally complete before the discussion gets down to business. Quantify his world for him with scales and numbers that work in your interests, rather than allowing him to establish a numerical framework that works against you.

Data – and the accompanying cues from the environment – define the framework for any professional sales negotiation and strongly determine its outcome. But relativity affects how we understand and interpret the entire context. Most commercial decisions have far too many aspects for a normal human being to take into account. That means we have to focus on a small number of important aspects in order to make decisions and to make pro-gress. We then exclude those aspects that are less conspicuous.

Whoever decides what is more important and less important establishes the frame within which the negotiation will proceed. The one who makes those decisions not only frames the negotiation in their own interests, but also has the opportunity to slip in elements under the radar later, because they consciously left them out of the negotiation. It is important that you influence – if not outright determine – the relative importance of what aspects you will discuss in a negotiation and also what aspects should *not* be discussed.

Relativity and prices: Shifting perception through anchoring

Let's get back to the suitcase experiment, but with a twist. Now we tell people that the suitcase weighs 25 pounds, and then give people another object to guess the weight of. Their estimates of the weight of that second object are much better than their estimates of the suitcase's weight in the absence of other information. People can detect noticeable differences in weight. With enough information, they can triangulate or home-in on an unknown weight with some accuracy. If we give people two objects whose weights are only slightly different, however, the likelihood is high that the person lifting them will perceive no difference at all.

But are you ready for another twist?

If we tell people that the suitcase weighs 30 pounds, and not 25 pounds, people will scale their numbers accordingly! They base their entire perceptions of weight on whatever number we give them. As long as that number is plausible – for example, we would never say 50 or 100 pounds for a 20-pound suitcase – the experiment works, and people accept our reference point at face value. System 1 dominates this exercise, because it is faster than System 2.

Assigning numbers in this manner is known as anchoring. In a business context, an anchor is a reference number that someone artificially yet purposefully sets to bias perception. Anchors constitute the reference set of information – usually numbers – that allows someone to quantify and scale a relative relationship (hot versus cold, heavy versus light, important versus unimportant). In that way, anchors facilitate decision making.

Think of anchoring this way: the first number cited in any discussion will have a strong influence on the last number cited in that same discussion.

The power of anchoring holds true in virtually any context, from casual conversations to the most complex sales negotiation. It is so essential to human psychology that more than 100,000 scientific articles deal with this phenomenon. The next two examples will demonstrate how anchoring influenced the responses of experiment participants and the level of charitable donations in a national appeal during an economic downturn.

Speaking of experiments, let's try one. On a piece of scrap paper, right down the last two digits of your mobile phone number, then put your local currency sign in front of it. If your phone number ends in 45 and you live in the United States, you would write $45. Now ask yourself whether the amount of money you wrote down is too much to pay for a box of Belgian chocolates. If your answer is 'yes', write down how much you would truly be willing to pay.

The concept of anchoring would imply that the first number you wrote down will influence both your initial assessment of how much the chocolates were worth as well as your personal willingness to pay. That influence occurs even though the last two digits of your phone number have nothing at all to do with the price of a box of Belgian chocolates. If that makes you sceptical or curious, read on.

The behavioural economist Dan Ariely once conducted a similar experiment together with MIT professor Drazen Prelec and Carnegie Mellon professor George Loewenstein. They asked 55 students to write down the last two digits of their social security numbers, express them in dollars, and then write that amount down next to six different products, including a cordless keyboard and mouse, a box of Belgian chocolates, and two bottles of wine.[1] They then asked the students whether they would pay that amount for the product, and then asked them to bid on each item. In other words, they asked for each student's maximum willingness to pay.

Ariely's analysis of the bids showed a clear correlation between the maximum willingness to pay and the last two digits of the student's social security number. In general, the higher the last two digits were, the higher the student's bid, independent of the product!

In 2015, the Singapore After Care Association (SACA) knew it would face some headwinds for its annual fundraising drive centred around its jubilee gala dinner to celebrate its 60th anniversary. To improve its odds, SACA sent out three different fundraising letters. One was its standard appeal. The second one used an additional tagline: 'We, here at SACA, would like to thank you for supporting our work in assisting ex-offenders and their families!' The third one used an alternate tagline: 'For a donation of $5,000, your company can make a difference in the lives of ex-offenders and their families.' Each letter went out to a group of 200 potential donors.[2]

Which letter do you think had the greatest effect? As you might expect by now, the third letter with the anchor proved to be the most successful, but the difference was impressive. That letter brought in 98% of the money that the SACA raised. The average donation was $7,150, and 43% of the donations exceeded $10,000.

These anecdotes all reaffirm the persistent power of anchoring. They also show the power of the illusion of price. Nothing at all – whether it is a car, a service, a meal, a coffee mug, or a speech – has an intrinsic, fixed value. The 'value' we attach to any product or service is both artificial and malleable. Whoever exercises the power in a negotiation can stretch and shape that number to serve whatever purposes they want. The only major limiting factors are the quality and credibility of the story and the reasoning ability of the buyer. The salesperson's aim is to keep System 1 engaged and flowing and keep System 2 functions at bay so that the buyer does not think of challenging the story.

The outcome of every negotiation is influenced, if not decided, by the price anchor. If the sales team doesn't decide on the scale and calibrate it, the buyers will, and that puts them in charge of the Invisible Game as well as the Visible Game. On the other hand, every time you open your mouth and utter the first number in a discussion, you are setting an anchor. That's why numbers you state need to be planned and purposeful. Anchors must be set by design, not by accident.

Anchoring requires discipline, situational awareness, and the courage to move first, as Situation 4.2 shows.

Situation 4.2: 'Wait and See'

My old boss always taught me to 'wait and see' until the other side shows their hand. He even showed me all kinds of anecdotal evidence and sayings to support his case. The best was a list called 'Rules for Fathers to Teach their Sons' that a friend of his had posted on Facebook. I admit that the list had some great common-sense advice.[3] Lesson #19 was 'A sport coat is worth 1,000 words.' My favourite, though, was Lesson #17: 'Never be afraid to ask out the best-looking girl in the room.'

But on this day, he stressed Lesson #4: 'In a negotiation, never make the first offer.'

Talk about conventional wisdom! Casting doubt on Lesson #4 would be tantamount to calling his entire list into question, never mind the value of the bond between a father and a son.

Maybe the rationale behind Lesson #4 is to see if the other side throws out a number that is strongly in your favour or will be easier to digest.

Or maybe the idea is to preserve a poker face as some kind of mastery or dominance over the situation. Perhaps that boss feels that any first move by a party must either be a concession or a moonshot?

We hope you know by now what we are going to say. Whoever makes the first move – regardless of whether the offer is serious – establishes a reference point and sets an anchor. That means two things. First, all subsequent discussions will proceed from that reference. Second, the party that cedes the first move to the other side is also ceding control.

What is the science behind this? The science behind this is relativity and anchoring. Our brains – guided spontaneously by System 1 – are hard-wired to make relative judgments. We have no biological system that can measure weight, temperature, or prices. Our evolutionary brain is attuned to the evaluation of *changes* rather than the evaluation of *absolutes*. Because we are insensitive to absolutes, we actively seek relativity or contrast. All contrasts in a negotiation are based on what we initially establish as a basis for contrast or comparison.

Adam D. Galinsky, now a professor at Columbia University, stressed the importance of a first offer as follows: 'By receiving the opening offer, the argument goes, you'll gain valuable information about your opponent's bargaining position and clues about acceptable agreements. This advice makes intuitive sense, but it fails to account for the powerful effect that first offers have on the way people think about the negotiation process. Substantial psychological research suggests that, more often than not, negotiators who make first offers come out ahead.'[4]

Galinsky and three co-authors later published research that shows how universal the first-offer effect is. Their findings revealed that the first-offer effect 'remains remarkably robust across cultures and multi-issue negotiations. Overall, these results reveal that moving first can benefit negotiators across many organizational and personal situations.'[5]

Our recommendation: Make the first move! Also take advantage of opportunities to put the price into relation in order to establish the contextual references. You might say that a new piece of equipment costs 'less than you spend on coffee for your office' or you might surround an offer with very expensive offers in order to elevate the other side's price perception.

What have we learned in Part I?

Behavioural economics, psychology, and neuroscience tell us that sales are won or lost on illusions. Thus, all business success and all profitability depend on how well you master the illusions of sales instead of letting them master you. In that regard, how can you become a better illusionist?

This is not science for science's sake. It is applying science to have more impact. The key to becoming a better illusionist is literally all in your brain, which works on two tracks: the quick intuitive System 1 and the slower analytical System 2. Think of System 1 as our untapped natural form of machine learning that we have had within ourselves all along. It improves as it gets more patterns and data to work with. That is what makes System 1 a powerful tool. But without the influence of System 2 – and reading this book is a System 2 process – your System 1 is prone to generate illusions and leave you vulnerable to uncertainty in a changing world.

The concepts we have introduced so far should give you greater confidence that you can gain an edge and improve your sales performance. The data side is important (that is our System 2) but mastering System 1 is also equally important for successful selling.

System 1 has ensured the survival of our species, but it is a double-edged sword. It does a massive amount of processing for us, but we still need to impose judgment on it. That is why we are still cavepeople despite the designer clothes. If salespeople fail to recognize System 1's abilities to serve as a trustworthy early-warning system and a powerful autopilot, they become vulnerable to the illusions of stability and success. On the other hand, when salespeople expand their comfort zones by continually seeking new experiences, they build a highly attuned, very responsive System 1 with powerful situational awareness.

The business world has focused so much on data science and information technology (IT) at the expense of what happens on the psychological side, which is just as hard a science as the others and can also have a greater impact. This area has been underinvested and hasn't had the huge emphasis that data science and IT have enjoyed.

To wrap up Part I, we would also like you to look at that piece of paper we asked you to prepare at the end of the Introduction. Knowing what you know now, based on what you have read in Part I, what would you do differently? And what would you continue to do, but with more confidence? Take your time before proceeding with Part II.

By now you may have identified some of your own nuggets of conventional wisdom that need replacement or revision. Feel free to jot those down and make your own set of sticky notes.

Part II

Playing Defence and the Power of 'No'

Imagine you are at a wine tasting with an expert sommelier. She starts with a few samples that she describes as mass market, because they are available in most liquor stores. Then she starts with the surprises.

First comes a glass from one of her vineyard's finest wines of recent years. You and the other guests have now entered an entirely different realm of taste and sophistication. For the finale, she brings out some rare bottles of red wine from the vineyard owner's exclusive private collection. Each guest had the option to buy one of those bottles at the end of the night for $550.

As you swirled the $550 wine in the glass and took the first sip, you are overwhelmed with the taste. You look to your companion, who nods and whispers 'this might be the best wine I have ever had!' You are anticipating another round of questions from the sommelier about the bouquet and the special flavour accents, but her next question catches you completely off guard.

'How did that price taste?' she asked.

People generally don't think that prices have a taste. Price is only a number, right? Even the Cambridge Dictionary defines price simply as the amount of money we exchange for something. Yet, several scientific studies over the past two decades – backed up by business experience – have solidly demonstrated that prices trigger intense sensory and emotional experiences in both buyers and sellers. These effects are deeper – and also more universal – than one could ever imagine by thinking of prices narrowly as mere numbers representing amounts of money.

Those last two statements may sound far-fetched. By the end of Part II, however, we expect that you will not only take those statements for granted, but also have practical ideas on how to make them cornerstones of your negotiation strategies. But there is work to be done. Salespeople cannot steer prices until they understand how prices steer people, and that includes yourself, not just the buyers.

Let's return to the wine-tasting. What would your reaction be if you found out that the sip of the $550 wine came not from the vintner's private cellar, but from a $55 bottle of wine you had tried earlier in the evening? You would probably feel shocked, upset, misled, and ripped off. But your inclination to mistake an affordable bottle of wine for one that costs 10 times as much would not surprise Antonio Rangel's Neuroeconomics Laboratory at the California Institute of Technology (CalTech).[1] One team led by his former post-doc student Hilke Plassmann used magnetic resonance imaging (MRI) to understand how people's brains respond to the combination of a sip of wine and a price level.[2]

They told the respondents they would be sampling five types of Cabernet Sauvignon, each with a different price point: $5, $10, $35, $45, and $90 per bottle. In reality, the wines priced at $5 and $45 were identical, as were the $10 wine and the $90 wine. The researchers found two clear positive correlations, one in the self-reporting from the respondents and one in the MRI scans. As the price points increased, the respondents reported a more pleasurable tasting experience, but the scans told an even more eye-opening story. They revealed that higher prices were accompanied by stronger activity in a brain area called the medial orbitofrontal cortex. This is important, because the medial orbitofrontal cortex becomes more active when people experience pleasant odours or tastes.

These results indicate that our brains translate a higher price on a bottle of wine into an enhanced sensory experience. The prices we see exert a strong influence on the pleasure we feel, but that is only one of the aspects of the behavioural, psychological, and neuroscientific power of prices.

The overarching concept behind the effect of prices on the taste of wine is the price-quality heuristic.[3] In its simplest form, it means that higher prices signal higher quality, while lower prices signal lower quality. Buyers use these relative relationships to make judgments about the quality of a product and whether they should purchase it.

Have you ever stepped back for a moment and asked yourself what a 'price' really is?

We are not talking about that simplistic Cambridge Dictionary definition of price that we cited above. We define a price as an arbitrary association between a product – including its stories and context – and a number. Think back to our discussion in Chapter 4 about the illusion of numbers. The reason we say 'arbitrary association' is that as human beings, we have no natural scale or meter to tell us what a price number means. That is what the suitcase experiment demonstrated. We don't have fixed barcode scanners hard-wired in our brains, in the same way we don't have built-in scales, or thermometers.

What we do have are ranges of sensations and impulses. Each of us can stick a foot in a swimming pool and tell immediately if we think the water is cold, hot, or just right. Our brains and bodies then respond accordingly, but we can't describe those sensations with numbers until we have reference points and context. That's why the recommended water temperature for a swimming competition is not simply warm, but rather 28 degrees Celsius. Similarly, we can infer the usefulness of special chemicals for water treatment through great stories or first-hand experience, but we can't have a 'number' conversation about water treatment chemicals until someone assigns a scale to that quality, such as a 'good' reference price of €100 per jug.

To show just how arbitrary these scales and their numbers are, that same conversation about swimming pools in the United States would put those reference points at 82 degrees Fahrenheit for the ideal water and $110 per jug for the chemicals to treat it. The numbers that represent prices have no intrinsic, absolute meaning on their own. They derive their meaning from the context that the seller provides and the associations that the buyer makes.

A team led by Brian Knutson of Stanford University showed that our brains make these associations and react to prices even before we consciously decide to make a purchase. When Knutson and his team used functional MRI to track people's purchase decisions as a function of price, their findings suggested that 'activation of distinct brain regions related to anticipation of gain and loss precedes and can be used to predict purchasing decisions'.[4] In other words, what buyers say about a price and what they really think and feel are two distinct things, and the latter one is often the more powerful of the two.

Steering those feelings to your advantage is one secret to playing defence and offence in a sales negotiation. Kai uncovered this phenomenon in his own research, in what the international media came to refer to as the 'Starbucks study'. One could safely assume that Starbucks sets its prices based on the value perception of its customers, just as it selects flavours based on their taste perceptions. After all, it has achieved spectacularly successful market entry in many places, including Europe, where Kai conducted his studies.

Think back to the research Kai described in the Introduction. The respondent's delayed responses and comments made him think that there was much more going on inside the respondent's mind than her simple yes-or-no responses to price points Kai revealed. In their 'Starbucks study' Kai and his team showed respondents the same cup of Starbucks coffee at different price points and also asked the participants to respond to the respective price with words such as cheap or expensive.[5] By tracking the brain waves of the respondents, they noticed that people quickly dismissed prices far outside reasonable boundaries, such as 10 cents or €10 per cup, but when the prices moved into a reasonable range, the optimal price worked out to €2.40 per cup.

What makes that finding astounding, however, is that the prevailing price for that cup of Starbucks coffee in the respondents' hometown was only €1.80, or 25% lower than the price that customers would find acceptable based on their brain waves. In numerous follow-up studies with companies such as PepsiCo, Kai demonstrated that the brain-based measurements vastly outperform traditional questionnaire-based methods for estimating a customer's willingness to pay. In the case of PepsiCo, traditional explicit pricing research predicted a revenue loss of 33% if the company raised the price for a pack of Lays Potato Chips in the Turkish market by 0.25 Turkish Lira. In contrast, the neuroscience approach predicted a revenue decline of only 9% following the price increase. PepsiCo implemented the price increase and incurred a revenue loss of 7%, far closer to that which the neuroscience approach had predicted.[6]

Chapter 5

Price = Maths + Story

We would not be surprised if someone is thinking right now: 'I don't sell wine and I don't sell coffee, so what does all this science have to do with me?'

To answer that question, we turn first to Nobel Prize winners George Akerlof (2001) and Robert Schiller (2013), who wrote a book together in 2009 called, *Animal Spirits: How Human Psychology Drives the Economy, and Why It Matters for Global Capitalism*. While they focus on macroeconomics, their comments on the importance of psychological aspects such as trust, fairness, and confidence are just as salient for day-to-day business. They write that these aspects 'are real motivations for real people. They are ubiquitous. The presumption of mainstream macroeconomics that they have no important role strikes us as absurd.'[1]

In other words, behavioural economics, psychology, and neuroscience apply to anyone who is selling, buying, or negotiating. We are all humans and thus subject to the same forces and effects. The concepts we have described so far – and the ones we will introduce throughout the rest of Parts II and III – reflect natural human tendencies with respect to prices and buying decisions. While some of our specific recommendations apply more to salespeople in larger organizations, most will apply just as much to independent professionals and individual business owners. They apply regardless of the industry, product, or service or the size of your business.

For a long time, classical economics ignored those universal tendencies, preferring instead to view our species as *homo economicus:* the efficient, economizing individuals who always act rationally in their own self interests. *Homo economicus* is the perfect incarnation of System 2, but many groundbreaking insights from the past few decades have exposed *homo economicus* as an incomplete and flawed model. More than half of the managers in the Swedish survey we cited in Chapter 1 said that intuition either partially or completely guides their business decisions. The Austrian economist Ludwig von Mises once wrote, 'It did not escape even the classical economists that the economizing individual as a party engaged in trade does not always and cannot always remain true to the principles governing the businessman, that he is not omniscient, that he can err, and that, under certain conditions, he even prefers his comfort to a profit-making business.'[2]

The magazine *The Atlantic* went one step further in an article with the headline 'Richard Thaler wins the Nobel in economics for killing *homo economicus.*' The article claimed that 'Thaler's career has been a lifelong war on *homo economicus*, that mythical species of purely rational hominids who dwell exclusively in the models of classical economic theory.'[3] Doubts about the predominance of rational economic thinking predates Thaler and others by several decades. In an effort to describe how people's emotional decisions can move markets, John Maynard Keynes coined the term 'animal spirits' in 1936, the same phrase that Akerlof and Schiller co-opted for their book.[4]

Homo economicus lingers as an undead creature, still casting some influence, but no longer viewed as the dominant or even all-powerful force. That means that purely rational beings are nowhere to be found on either side of a Zoom call or around a business negotiating table. Let's keep that in mind as we leave the world of wine and coffee and look at a story about prices in a large corporation.

Glasswhere, an international supplier of laboratory equipment, wanted to launch a line of heavy-duty chemical gloves to complement its existing assortment of lab materials.[5] The managers didn't know a lot about the market for gloves, so they turned to catalogues and websites to find the prevailing list prices and get some orientation. That is when they hatched the idea for an experiment.

Working together with a couple of its leading distributors, Glasswhere conducted in-market tests with different price points to determine the launch price for the rollout. These tests resemble the CalTech wine experiment, but instead of self-reporting their pleasure with the gloves at a given price point, the lab-equipment buyers expressed their satisfaction (and presumably, their pleasure) by paying actual money for the gloves. Glasswhere learned that, on average, its own branded gloves could command a premium of at least 10% above what Ergz, the market leader, was charging. Focus groups and small-scale surveys in other markets confirmed the findings.

What makes these findings remarkable? The gloves Glasswhere tested under their own brand name were not only worth 10% more than the gloves made by Ergz, the market leader and their new main competitor. They actually *were* Ergz's gloves. This experiment underscores the interconnection between prices and the stories behind them. In this case, the brand carried the story. Brands serve as a powerful shorthand for the context that a company creates about itself, reinforced by the first-hand experience of customers. Stories and prices are inseparable in any buying decision, and there will always be irresistible combinations of them.

In essence, the brand acts like a magic combination of words and images that is capable of triggering positive sensations in buyers. This applies equally to B2B products as it does to a pair of athletic shoes, a fashionable handbag, or even restaurants, which are fascinating real-life laboratories for understanding the power of the System 1 aspects of pricing. Writing about the brand-name power of Scottish chef Gordon Ramsay, *The Guardian* said that 'Ramsay realized the opinions of foodies didn't matter. If his profile was high enough, if he spent enough airtime pushing his brand values of fanatical attention to detail and uncompromising standards, his presence in the kitchen made no difference to the number of people flocking to his restaurants.'[6] People bought and tasted Ramsay's brand, not the food he personally cooked.

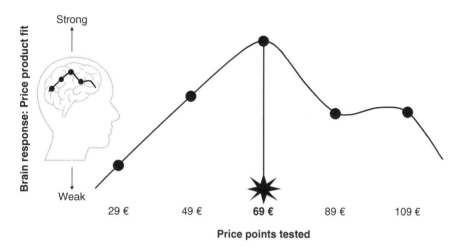

Figure 5.1 Prices are emotional triggers that are inseparable from stories. The 'feel-good' price is the highest price that still elicits a pleasant, positive response in the buyer's mind

All of this cutting-edge science supports our important claim that price is a sensorial, emotional, and thus ultimately a neurobiological experience for all humans. No matter what product or service you are selling or buying, the price is so much more than a mere number. Prices are the outcomes of stories with the power to steer the full range of human emotions: fear, anger, happiness, elation, euphoria, disappointment, resentment, jealousy, and dread, to name a few. Prices can make you feel pleasure and pain.

In Figure 5.1 the 'feel-good' price for the buyer is €69. However, traditional sales training – derived from the classic conventions about how prices work – almost guarantees that a salesperson will fall short of the feel-good price, and in many cases drift even further away from it as the customer relationship continues. The reason is that this classical training overemphasizes System 2 and largely ignores System 1. It operates under the classic definition of 'brain power', which is the intellectual capacity to solve problems. This definition neglects the other dimensions of brain power – and often the predominant ones – which include situational awareness, emotions, and the refined intuition that allows someone to turn intuitive behaviours into intentional ones.

The overarching conclusion from numerous experiments – both in well-controlled studies and semi-formal observations – is that these two sides of brain power exist within every buyer–seller relationship and likewise within every negotiation between those two parties.

These two sides also exist within the stories themselves. Of course, the stories include the differentiation and value arguments that derive from your System 2 activity, but often overlook the pre-conscious and emotional stories embedded invisibly in the negotiation process. A price may ultimately be a number, but the creation and defence of that number – based on the full forceful combination of System 1 and System 2 – is what makes pricing an essential skill to master in the Invisible Game.

Chapter 6

Psyched Up or
Psyched Out?

Repeated success in sales negotiations requires not only situational awareness and the knowledge of System 1 and System 2. You also need the power to change your own responses to situations, and at the same time, influence how others respond.

What kind of intuitive yet intentional responses would you like to have? After all, everyone wonders about 'what if. . .?' questions from time to time. What would you do if you won the lottery? What would you do if you won a prestigious award? The situations are not always fun or positive ones. What would you do if you needed to make a speech in front of 1,000 people after winning that award? Or far worse, what would you do if an intruder entered your home in the middle of the night?

The truth is that most people have absolutely no idea how they would really respond in those situations, regardless of what they might speculate or claim. This is especially true when the person has never experienced that situation.

Now imagine that you are out for a leisurely walk on a sunny afternoon and a stranger suddenly collapses nearby. What would you do? Kai's parents had an opportunity to find out on a late summer day in 2020. When a middle-aged woman fell unconscious near them, the woman's sister froze in panic. In the first critical moments, everyone else seemed paralyzed with inaction, including Kai's mother.

Kai's father, however, sprang into action.

His quick response and actions ultimately saved the woman's life by keeping her stable until an emergency team arrived. 'Make them safe, call in the emergency, start with heart massage, and every second counts . . . that's the way it's set in the back of my mind', he told a local radio station.[1]

Everyone's immediate actions on that sidewalk in Aspach, Germany were governed by System 1, but in the case of Kai's father, these actions reflected a considerable amount of training, to the point of programming. He had spent years as a voluntary firefighter and afterwards kept his responses sharp with Red Cross training.

Soldiers, actors, professional athletes, and medical professionals are prominent examples of people who exhibit strong and positive reactions in high-pressure situations that others with less practice, training, or experience could not summon. This type of programming is deep-seated within the mental machinery. The complexity of the task at hand as well as the presence of others can elicit and enhance these pre-programmed responses. A University of Michigan psychologist named Robert Zajonc tested that theory by confronting 72 participants in a study with four challenges: sprint in a straight line with and without a crowd present, and run through a maze, likewise with and without a crowd present.

The straight-line sprint served as the proxy for a simple challenge, while the maze served as the complex – and presumably more challenging – test for the participants. The resulting academic paper by Zajonc and his colleagues claimed clearly, 'runway performance was facilitated when compared to performance . . . in solitary conditions' while 'maze performance was impaired'.[2] The team therefore concluded that, 'the mere presence of conspecifics is a source of general arousal that enhances the emission of dominant responses.'[3] For any given challenge, every single creature will exhibit what is known as a dominant response. These are stereotypical System 1 responses, hard-wired in our brains, independent of what we might claim or say when we discuss stressful situations hypothetically.

To put Zajonc's findings into plain English: if a crowd watches you do a simple, habitual, or routine task, the chances are that you will perform better than if you did the task in isolation. In terms of a dominant response, it means that the presence of observers – a partisan crowd at a sports event, colleagues at a meeting, or attendees at a conference – will enhance your performance of your ingrained or intuitive tasks. You are psyched up, not psyched out.

How universal and pervasive is the idea of a dominant response? When the dominant response of almost everyone on that summer day in Germany was to panic, Kai's father's dominant response was to offer first aid. Think back also to the 'blackout moment' of baseball outfielder Adam Eaton that we described in Part I. In a do-or-die final game, he saw a pitch coming and told himself, 'No, don't swing!' but his dominant response was to swing anyway. His successful hit helped his team win the 2019 World Series.

Perhaps the most fascinating aspect of Zajonc's experiment takes us back to 'animal spirits,' the term coined by Keynes and used by Akerlof and Schiller for their book title. That's because Zajonc didn't conduct that experiment with people. He conducted it with cockroaches.

Obviously, we are not trying to equate salespeople with cockroaches. But challenges in the business world likewise elicit dominant responses from all participants, and a sales negotiation is no exception. The responses are so deeply rooted and hard-wired that we share those basic elements with the world's simplest social animals.

You recall that in Part I, we explained why salespeople should make the first move in a negotiation. This defies the conventional wisdom that the sales team should 'wait and see' what the buyers expect for a price. The problem is that a 'wait-and-see' stance allows the purchasing team to set a price anchor that frames the entire negotiation. That puts the selling team at a disadvantage that can often be insurmountable.

Let's envision a sales negotiation and assume that the sales team makes its first offer. In that case, the most common next step is for the buyer to ask for a lower price. When that happens – as it almost inevitably does – the path and the outcome of the entire negotiation can hinge on the dominant response your brain brings forth.

What will that dominant response be?

Imagine that you could say 'no' to those requests immediately, with confidence and without hesitation or reservation. You are psyched up, not psyched out. Wouldn't that be a great superpower to have? Imagine having the same kind of immediate, powerful, and trained reaction as a paramedic, soldier, or athlete, when a customer asks for a lower price, a discount, or some other form of concession.

Motivating you to develop and maintain 'no' as your dominant response to discount requests is one of our primary objectives in Part II. It is an essential aspect of playing defence in the Invisible Game. Ingraining that habit will prevent you from drifting even further away from the 'feel-good' price in the buyer's minds, as shown in Figure 5.1. The same techniques will also enable you take other steps – comfortably, confidently, and consistently – to close deals at prices that are much closer to the feel-good price by implementing price increases and price adjustments. Those are essential aspects of playing offence in the Invisible Game, and we explore the techniques for offence in Part III.

Chapter 7

Paying the Price of 'Yes'

Why is the dominant response of many salespeople 'yes' when a customer asks for a discount or a lower price? Why is that dominant response so difficult to change?

There are many presumably positive reasons why salespeople make concessions and agree to offer discounts. Discounting can help close a deal quickly, make customers happy, and increase sales volumes and revenue. Discounting can be a very effective tool to counter competitive pressures, whether real or anticipated.

The acceptance of discounting as a useful tactic may also be a halo effect from what salespeople experience as private consumers when they receive discounts, coupons, or free trials.[1] The underlying assumption is that if such tactics enhance the personal satisfaction they derive from private purchases, such concessions could engender the same goodwill with customers in a business-related sale. Over time, their own personal experience unwittingly reinforces an urge to respond favourably whenever a client asks for a discount. Hence, salespeople's untrained dominant response is to yield to the natural inclination to say 'yes'. It will remain their response until they change it consciously.

The studies from Zajonc offer insights into how external conditions can determine how appropriate and how successful the untrained dominant response will be. Whenever the dominant response is the appropriate course of action, it implies that the task is easier or has less at stake. Conversely, if the appropriate response is different from or antithetical to the dominant response – such as when a 'no' is required to a request for a lower price – it implies that the task is more difficult. This difficulty may be amplified when the task involves high stakes.

To put it bluntly: when your untrained System 1 response kicks in, it exposes you to too much compromise. The more complex, challenging, or stressful a situation is, the greater the chances are that you will not perform as well, or even screw up the task entirely, with potentially permanent consequences. You end up psyched out, not psyched up.

Scrutiny or observation can artificially boost the amount of stress in a social situation. Psychologists refer to this phenomenon as social facilitation. Imagine what this means for the performance of salespeople working in large corporations, where complexity is the norm. In their sales negotiations, the money and the management fill the role of social facilitation, heightening the pressure and enhancing the effects. There are thousands of dollars at stake for a salesperson in terms of salary, commission, and bonuses. Often millions more are at stake in terms of revenue and profit for the company the salesperson works for. Attempts by the purchasers to impose artificially tight deadlines or otherwise throw off the sales team increase the stress. The buyers are trying to ensure that their request for lower prices will draw a 'yes' from the salespeople when the answer should clearly be 'no' or at least 'wait.'

Figure 7.1 shows how these forces apply to such sales negotiation. Think of it as a representation of the factors that can literally make your blood pressure rise. The risk of a bad outcome from a 'yes' increases if any of these conditions exist: there is a large financial commitment at stake, the negotiation is complex (perhaps involving multiple products, terms and

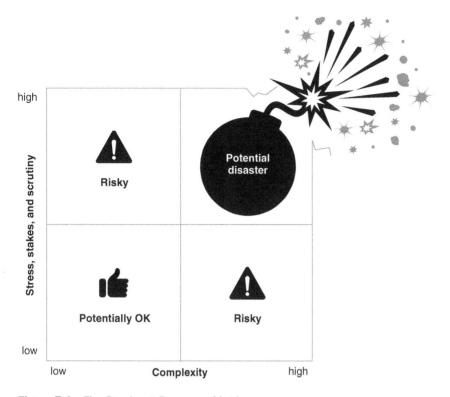

Stress, stakes, and scrutiny

Risky

Potential disaster

Potentially OK

Risky

low

low   **Complexity**   high

Figure 7.1 The Dominant Response Matrix

conditions, timeframes, and business units), or the negotiation is taking place under unexpected or high stress (limited time, team mismatch, limited resources). These factors conspire to trigger a person's dominant response. The decisive question is whether that person will be psyched up or psyched out by these stress factors.

There are occasions when the buyer asks for a relatively innocuous concession, such as the waiving of a modest fee. The exchange is only between you and the buyer, the amount is so small that it is almost immaterial to your business, and the decision requires no escalation or additional input from your side. Such situations are most likely in the lower left quadrant of Figure 7.1.

A tense and complex negotiation with your largest key account – under an extreme and unexpected time pressure – could fall into that upper-right quadrant. If the stress, complexity, scrutiny, and potential business impact are all high, then saying 'yes' to a discount request in such a negotiation can lead to a disaster with negative consequences that are either permanent or will require tremendous effort to undo. The outcome of that negotiation could have consequences across your company's entire value chain.

A salesperson's immediate 'yes' is always a decision that limits or even eliminates their room to manoeuvre. They lose the opportunity to see if everything else makes sense in the current context and to weigh other viable options besides a discount. Having 'no' as the dominant response will buy the sales team time to see if a discount might in fact make sense. The team can step back, apply its System 2 judgment, and come back with either a reaffirmation of the 'no' or a counterproposal to the discount. Saying 'no' also has immediate effects on the purchasing team. One of those effects is to reinforce or re-establish your anchor by drawing attention to it again.

Figure 7.2 If your goal is to achieve the 'feel-good' price – the price that matches the most intense response in the buyer's brain – you undermine yourself every time you say 'yes' to a discount request

If your goal is to achieve the 'feel-good' price, you undermine yourself every time you say 'yes' to a discount request. That underscores why 'no' should become the dominant response. As Figure 7.2 shows, the dominant response of 'yes' causes the team to drift further and further away from the feel-good price.

What *homo economicus* says about prices and discounts

Why are discounts as risky or even disastrous, as the Dominant Response Matrix in Figure 7.1 shows? To answer this question, we turn briefly to System 2 and its representative, *homo economicus*.

Mainstream behavioural economics may have declared *homo economicus* dead, but we prefer to say undead. The ghost of that rational being still haunts the halls of most businesses, pervading everything from strategic planning to price setting. It has plenty to say about the mechanics and consequences of discounting and, from a purely mathematical standpoint, the ghost is correct. So it is worthwhile to review the classical side of discounts before we dive any deeper into more of the behavioural, psychological, and neuroscientific aspects.

Let's start with the textbook role of corporate salespeople. Sales should influence the purchasing decision in such a way that the final choice is their company's desired product at a targeted price. There is no shortage of fancy economic theories and complicated equations – and nowadays, AI-driven algorithms – to help people find the right price. Prices also come in many flavours and forms: target, ceiling, floor, equilibrium, walkaway, average, gross, and net. If you have enough time and enough data, you can find the *optimal* price by plotting supply, demand, and cost curves and measuring price elasticities by customer segment. That is the conventional view of pricing that you will find in any textbook, university class, or training programme.

Situation 7.1 looks at how that conventional view plays out in a real-life selling situation.

Situation 7.1: They're putting my business up for bid!

My key account is considering a competitive bid on their total purchase spend. I am their largest supplier. That would put my entire current business at risk. In order to prevent that from happening and to keep my sales, I will offer the customer a discount based on my current sales. My thought is to offer them a 15% discount to keep the business and potentially expand it so that I can achieve my revenue targets. A 15% discount means that I would need to increase volume by 15% to keep revenue constant, right?

What is the science behind this? The science required here is break-even analysis, which is a pure System 2 exercise. The question is how much additional volume you would need to sell to make that discount worthwhile financially, and what the overall financial consequences are. Maintaining the business is important, but what is the cost?

As Table 7.1 shows, there is never a one-to-one correspondence between a discount percentage and the percentage increase in volume required to

Table 7.1 Volume increase required to keep revenue constant after a discount. (All figures rounded to the nearest full amount)

Discount	Revenue in US$	Unit price in US$	Volume	
			Units	Change
0%	10,000	100	100	0%
3%	10,000	97	103	3%
5%	10,000	95	105	5%
10%	10,000	90	111	11%
15%	**10,000**	**85**	**118**	**18%**
18%	10,000	82	122	22%
20%	10,000	80	125	25%
25%	10,000	75	133	33%

compensate for it. For a given discount in percentage terms, the required percentage increase in volume will always be higher.

If a salesperson offers a discount of 15% per unit, revenue will decline unless the customer buys at least 18% more units. That is the amount of additional volume you would need to sell just to keep your revenue constant.

These facts become even more compelling when we take the situation one step further. Let's assume that your product has a gross margin of 20% right now, at a price of 100 before you offer any discounts.[2] We will even assume that no matter what discount you offer, you will succeed in selling enough additional volume to keep revenue constant. How strong will the effect be on profit? That is what Table 7.2 shows.

In our working example, this means that you sold 18% more volume and kept revenue constant after the 15% discount. Congratulations, but look what happens to profit! That discount of 15% will decrease profits by 72%, even though you worked hard and succeeded in keeping your revenue constant. The steeper the discount is, the more the profit level plummets.

What is our recommendation? Understand the consequences of any discount action before a negotiation even begins. The ghost of *homo economicus* is not only making a compelling financial argument, but it is stating

Table 7.2 How discounts affect profit, assuming no revenue loss after a discount and constant unit cost. (All figures rounded to the nearest full amount)

Dis-count	Revenue in US$	Price in US$	Volume		Unit Cost in US$	Profit in US$	
			Units	Change		Amount	Change
0%	10,000	100	100	0%	80	2,000	0%
3%	10,000	97	103	3%	80	1,760	−12%
5%	10,000	95	105	5%	80	1,600	−20%
10%	10,000	90	111	11%	80	1,120	−44%
15%	**10,000**	**85**	**118**	**18%**	**80**	**560**	**−72%**
18%	10,000	82	122	22%	80	240	−88%
20%	10,000	80	125	25%	80	–	−100%
25%	10,000	75	133	33%	80	(640)	−132%

mathematical facts. No matter how you tweak the initial gross margin percentage in our example in Tables 7.1 and 7.2, you can't escape the fact that lower prices – in the form of discounts – lead to lower profits. That is how discounts become the source of risk and damage, as the Dominant Response Matrix shows. Saying 'yes' – the salesperson's path of least resistance – is a toll road, and a costly one at that.

Saying 'yes' to a discount is like flashing your money in public and wondering later why someone picked your pocket. A willingness to discount makes you a prime target.

To take one final look, let's calculate the amount of volume you would need to sell to keep profit constant. The starting situation is the same: a 20% gross margin at the current price. Offering a discount of 15% means that you would need to *quadruple* sales volume in order to keep absolute profit at the same level.

Table 7.3 Volume uplift required to keep profit constant after a discount. (All figures except volume change rounded to the nearest full amount)

Dis-count	Revenue in US$	Price in US$	Volume		Unit Cost in US$	Unit Margin in US$	Profit in US$
			Units	Change			
0%	10,000	100	100	0.0%	80	20	2,000
3%	11,446	97	118	17.6%	80	17	2,000
5%	12,635	95	133	33.3%	80	15	2,000
10%	18,000	90	200	100.0%	80	10	2,000
15%	**34,000**	**85**	**400**	**300.0%**	**80**	**5**	**2,000**
18%	82,000	82	1000	900.0%	80	2	2,000

Why it is so hard to say 'no' to discounts

Why would people offer discounts when it is indisputable how much financial damage they can do?

There are many explanations for that behaviour. An article in *Entrepreneur* magazine declared that discounting, 'is like an addiction. You're going to have to break the negotiating habit cold turkey'.[3] Management and pricing specialists typically cite several reasons why salespeople surrender to the pressures to offer a discount.[4] The reasons include a bad price and segment structure, a bad value story, poor training, poor management oversight, and a misaligned incentive system. In other words, these experts are alleging that salespeople default to discounts as their dominant response because they lack the right guidance, the right data-driven lines of argument, the right rules, and the right incentives. The absence of these four things creates a powerful vacuum that practically sucks the salesperson down the path of least resistance.

In turn, these presumed rationales for discounting form the basis of the solutions that companies undertake to avoid the dangers of discounts. The common denominator among these solutions is to barricade the path of resistance, or at least clog it up. The thinking is that if the company drowns the salesperson in more facts, applies more force, demands more paperwork, or conducts more oversight, then salespeople will stop giving money away in the form of discounts and lower prices.

Analogous to castle walls in the Middle Ages, these administrative burdens and rules are intended to serve as barriers to protect a company's profit pool from intrusion. These procedures can range from submission forms, to multiple signoffs, to escalation procedures. Some companies implement additional oversight and various combinations of carrots and sticks to cajole salespeople into being arch-defenders of their company's price recommendations, price negotiation guidelines, and bottom lines. These solutions boil down to one thing: impose additional burdens on salespeople, even if they represent 'non-productive activity that creates an additional administrative burden and imposes a deadweight loss'.[5]

In the Old Economy, these types of hierarchical and procedural burdens may indeed protect profitability for a company in the short term. That short-term success convinces managers that these tactics are useful ways to 'solve' the discount problem, but all they do is address some symptoms of why salespeople discount. They do nothing to address the root cause, and paradoxically, they can even make matters worse.

The last idea we'll discuss from the *homo economicus* camp, appropriately, involves money. In addition to or instead of imposing burdens, some companies try to change their incentive systems, with the belief that more money is the answer: 'Incent[ivize] salespeople to sell at a higher price and they will.'[6] That seems like the pure definition of a rational trade-off, right? These incentive scheme changes can be blunt and straightforward, such as making commissions inversely proportional to any discounts a salesperson offers. Other such systems are quite elaborate, involving points schemes, but there are numerous studies that cast doubt on the effectiveness of additional money as a means of changing behaviour, especially over the medium and long term.

The reason why companies try to use more facts, more force, and more money to 'solve' the discount problem is that they haven't recognized the root cause. Salespeople don't say 'yes' to discount requests because they lack enough knowledge, rules, or compensation. They say 'yes' because that is their untrained dominant response to the buyers' questions.

The good news – and the basis for the remaining chapters in Part II – is that behavioural economics, psychology, and neuroscience can enable salespeople to retrain their dominant responses and cure the act of discounting.

Chapter 8

Overcoming the Fear of 'No'

We mentioned earlier that the Cambridge Dictionary defines price as the amount of money we exchange for something, but the dictionary contains a second primary definition of price: 'the unpleasant results that you must accept or experience for getting or doing something'.[1] In other words, a price is also a burden. This second definition of price – equally valid as the first – also matters in sales negotiations: Who pays that price for the outcome? Who bears the burdens?

This question is usually overlooked, to the detriment of salespeople, their products, and their companies. The presumptive solutions described in the previous chapter impose an additional burden on salespeople in order to make it harder for them to say 'yes'. But what if we define the problem differently. Instead of trying to make it harder for them to say 'yes', why not make it easier for them to say 'no'? That difference sounds esoteric, but from a practical and behavioural standpoint, the two phrasings could hardly be further apart.

There are two primary reasons why making a 'no' easier is a better approach than imposing additional burdens on salespeople in order to make a 'yes' harder. The first primary reason involves the mental and emotional aspects of discounting that the ghost of *homo economicus* doesn't acknowledge. Think back to the wine experiments and the price–quality heuristic. Prices have strong emotional effects and not merely financial ones. Similarly, there are forces within our brains that reinforce 'yes' as the untrained dominant response.

In larger companies, the administrative burdens of the conventional 'castle' solutions we described in Chapter 7 artificially impose an uncomfortable mental burden on salespeople. This is counterproductive, because rules often dare salespeople to find expedient ways to work around the rules and procedures to give the customers what they want. The rules encourage evasion rather than compliance.

Let's say a discount above 10% requires approval from sales management. Salespeople can circumvent that rule by staggering the discount (say, first 6% and then 4%) to stay under the threshold. Sometimes sales management takes the path of least resistance as well. When a salesperson ostensibly submits 20 pages of forms to defend a discount by sending an email at 11:30 a.m. and approval comes via email two minutes later, did anyone really read those forms? Finally, the 'castle' rules lead to unintended consequences in terms of how salespeople interpret the logic: if the salespeople are required to defend the discount by following burdensome rules, then the discount must be worth defending, right? This makes the dominant response of 'yes' even harder to dislodge.

Now let's get to the second primary reason why making 'no' easier is the better approach than making 'yes' harder. The New Economy, driven by rapid ongoing progress in digitalization, has thrived by flattening hierarchies and encouraging agility. Speed and agility are the new key success factors for any organization, regardless of size. Larger companies are changing their organizations to keep up with the agility of smaller competitors. These fast, agile organizations require self-steering teams that can learn continually. Responsibilities are migrating from the centre to the front lines, so that companies can act faster and be as close to their customers as possible.

Customers in turn expect to interact with people who are empowered and enabled, not with people who are hamstrung by unfavourable perceptions of slowness and bureaucracy. Who wants to negotiate with a salesperson who is constrained by extra rules and processes? The digital economy needs salespeople equipped with meaningful pricing autonomy. The establishment of barriers and elaborate internal processes is counterproductive. Fortifying those barriers and complicating the processes only make matters worse.

This is the practical argument for educating and training salespeople so that it is easier for them to say 'no' to requests for discounts or lower prices. This ability – this *trained* dominant response – will become increasingly important as end-to-end digitalization and process automation between companies create new standards for interaction. In this new world, salespeople will become involved primarily – and in many cases, only – at times of active decision making, which involves the kinds of judgment calls that a machine cannot make.

Boston Consulting Group (BCG) cited data that show that professional buyers, on average, complete 57% of their purchase process before they get in touch with a salesperson.[2] Such data clearly show that the role of the salesperson has fundamentally changed. In the Old Economy, salespeople pitched the product and provided basic information. In the New Economy, the buyers often have more information and advance knowledge than the salesperson could ever hope to provide them with. That means that salespeople should consider themselves to be influencers, not information providers.

The science behind 'yes'

If you want to become an agile, autonomous decision maker and influencer, one of the key prerequisites is to recognize and internalize what we said at the start of Part II: salespeople cannot steer prices until they understand how prices steer people. 'People' in that sense applies to everyone, but especially to the buyers and the salespeople themselves.

Making it easier to say 'no' means overriding or minimizing four universal phenomena which conspire to reinforce 'yes' as the dominant response:

1. Saying 'yes' is easy and fast, especially amidst resource constraints or artificial pressure.
2. It is easier to ignore inconvenient or uncomfortable facts than to embrace them.
3. Losing hurts more than winning excites, even when the spoils are equal.
4. Losing face or losing a relationship hurts more than losing money.

The simplicity of these statements belies just how deeply rooted and universal these effects are in human thinking. They are powerful and omnipresent, which means they have a material effect on the outcomes of any sales negotiations. Prices not only recalibrate value in the conventional, financial sense. Prices also alter the emotional intensity and spectrum within a negotiation, in the same way that a higher price changes the sensorial experience of sipping an otherwise ordinary glass of wine.

There are also forces that act upon the buyer's mind in a sales negotiation, and we will highlight a couple of important ones when we talk about playing offence for price adjustments and price increases in Part III. For now, we concentrate on what is going on within the salesperson's mind.

1. Saying 'yes' is easy and fast, especially in times of resource constraints or artificial pressure

Psychologically, a 'yes' provides the salesperson with immediate relief and resolution at an emotional level. This is especially true when a business comes under pressure to make a sale. If you want to make a customer happy, it is easy to believe that the most expedient means at your disposal – and in many cases, the only one – is to say 'yes' to a demand for a lower price. 'Yes' eliminates the fear and risk of losing a sale, because the negotiation is over.

By default, a 'yes' also reduces a corporate salesperson's workload. Saying 'no' might mean spending additional hours working on the problem, but there is also the issue of personal workload. Say 'yes' could mean getting a day off or making it to a child's event on time.

2. It is easier to ignore inconvenient or uncomfortable facts than to accept them

Imagine seeing an advertisement for a conference that claims to teach you how to cut your company's profits in half. The conference sponsor even sells merchandise such as t-shirts and mugs with the phrase 'Money Loser' printed on them in huge letters.

Would you race down to sales VP's office and ask for the budget to register for the conference and travel to the site? Of course you wouldn't. No one in their right mind would sign up for a conference with that topic.

Yet, every day companies sign contracts that guarantee discounts that essentially accomplish the same effect. Think back to the Table 7.3. If your company achieves a margin of 20% at current prices, offering a discount of 15% would cut profits by over 70%, even if that discount allowed you to sell enough additional volume to keep your revenue constant.

Why do we discount when we know the costs? Why do we do that, even when we can recite the counterarguments by heart and calculate the damage on the back of an envelope? As Bremen University professor Gerhard Roth explains, human beings want congruence between their experiences, beliefs, and actions – past, present, and future. Ideally, what we do right now should not only align with our massive treasure chest of past experiences, but also be something we can live with tomorrow.[3] We all need congruence between what we do in the outside world and how we want to see ourselves. Our previous experiences influence our decisions, even if we try consciously to diminish or dismiss them. Not everyone is living in the past, but the past is living in everyone.

So when we encounter conflict instead of congruence, we experience a psychological force known as cognitive dissonance. This dissonance arises when salespeople understand the dire maths shown in the Tables 7.1, 7.2, and 7.3, but ignore the implications anyway, usually with an excuse like, 'growth will make up for the losses'. They ignore the fact that some markets do not have enough excess demand to allow the firm to break even after a discount. Offering a substantial discount virtually guarantees that the company will earn less money.

When we face the dilemma of needing to say 'no' but wanting to say 'yes,' System 2 and System 1 urge opposing courses of action. This leaves the salesperson with two basic options to create an alignment or congruence between action and attitude:

- **Change the action:** Choose the hard route by learning to say 'no' and learning to indulge in the feeling of having done the right thing.
- **Change the attitude:** Say 'yes' to the request and find some rationalization or justification that allows you to believe that 'yes' makes more sense than 'no'.

People find all sorts of ways to rationalize a 'yes', which is the untrained dominant response from System 1. Sometimes they think that the deal or the customer is 'strategic' without specifying what that strategy is. Sometimes they buy into the belief that the customer will reward the concession by buying more product in the future, even if the volume of the current deal remains unchanged.

The desire to rationalize can be so intense that some sales teams preplan their excuses as well as their pitches. People find comfort in knowing they can explain a bad outcome, should one occur, but there is a significant risk that these advance rationalizations become self-fulfilling prophecies. It is interesting that the English language uses the word 'rationalization' for our mental excuse-making machinery. The word implies that what happened – the unexpected or unfavourable outcome we are trying to cope with – was somehow irrational.

As we explained in Part I, the conflicts that play out between System 1 and System 2 are not rational versus irrational, but rather between two powerful forms of thought, each of which makes perfect sense in its own context. Each leads to desirable outcomes when we understand how they work and how to apply them.

The worst resolution of the cognitive dissonance is a change of attitude that turns the salesperson against his or her own company. The salesperson thinks, 'My company does not care about me. They don't pay me enough and they don't appreciate my work. So why should I work in their interests when I can put my self-interest and my own personal "profitability" first?' They feel better after offering the discount and can live with themselves, even if the 'yes' costs them some commission money. If a salesperson self-optimizes in a way that works against the employer's interests, that's a recipe for disaster.

Any 'yes' may seem like a one-off, but when someone changes their attitude, it virtually assures that will repeat that action. This is how one-time rationalizations become permanent ways of thinking, thus reinforcing the dominant response. There is a chicken–egg question regarding whether attitude determines action, or whether action determines attitude. For salespeople, the latter is often the case. The desire to say 'yes' prevails and over time can turn a rationalization into a doctrine.

3. Losing hurts more than winning excites, even when the spoils are equal

Here's a quiz that is more elaborate than our usual ones. Let's look at two events that salespeople will almost assuredly encounter if they are in business long enough. After you read the first event – but before you continue – immediately write down a few words to describe how you would feel if that happened to you. Perhaps you can recall a similar event in your own career.

Then read the second event and do the same.

Event A: A new client agrees to a sale valued at $500,000. You and your team log out of the conference call, satisfied and ready to celebrate. As you await the arrival of the formal purchase order, you already notify the rest of the company to arrange production and shipping timelines. Then two days later you wake up to an email from the head of the procurement team. She begins with a euphemism-filled explanation that there was a detailed review, some potential conflicts of interest and contractual matters, and so on, and then comes to the punch-in-the-gut line: you won't be getting a purchase order. The deal is off.

Now, quickly write down how you feel, before reading Event B. Once you have captured those initial thoughts, take a timeout and consider what happened and what your next steps might be. This will give you a System 1 and an initial System 2 perspective.

After that, you can proceed to Event B.

Event B: You and your team are renegotiating a $500,000 deal with a client whose business you had counted on for the current year. For the last three years, these meetings have been little more than rubber-stamp events, with perhaps a few changes at the margins but no threat to the ongoing relationship. This year, however, you leave the conference call feeling exhausted and deflated. After a drawn-out negotiation process that you think you have managed very well, you receive every possible signal that the client will not renew. Those $500,000 you counted on have essentially gone 'poof'. Before the postmortem even begins, you start drawing up plans on how to replace that sudden hole in your budget. Then two days later you wake up to an email from the head of the procurement team. He apologizes for being somewhat vague and evasive in the previous meeting, but they had some final internal obstacles to overcome. Then he comes to the punch-bowl line: you will be getting a fresh purchase order after all. The deal is still on!

Now quickly write down how you feel, both initially and after some thought. Then compare your responses to each event.

Behavioural science would predict that you probably felt angry, upset, ripped off, or humiliated by Event A, while you felt relieved, lucky, or perhaps happy by Event B. The fascinating thing about the stark differences between those lists is that from a purely financial standpoint, there is no difference between Event A and Event B.

In Event A, you thought you had sold an incremental $500,000 worth of business, then effectively lost that business a couple of days later. In Event B, you thought you were about to lose $500,000 from your planned revenue base, only to find out a few days later that you had retained your business. In both situations, the net financial effect is zero. Your revenue base is unchanged.

How you feel, however, is much different. The explanation lies in prospect theory, a set of concepts that earned Kahneman a Nobel Prize in 2002.[4] Prospect theory has practical applications for sales negotiations, because it helps to explain the way we assign probabilities to outcomes and the way we feel about those outcomes. People have a psychological or emotional 'zero point' that differs from their objective financial one. In this case, the order of the outcomes recalibrates the emotional zero point even though financial impact is zero.

4. Losing face or losing a relationship hurts more than losing money

A group of salespeople was asked to evaluate the current state of their relationships with the customers, seemingly drawn from a random list.[5] They used a 'stoplight' system: green meant that they were on good terms, the customer liked them, and vice versa. Negotiating deals with them usually went smoothly. Yellow meant that the relationship was neutral or fair, with both sides pushing for compromises that left neither side feeling disadvantaged. The salesperson viewed the customer as neither friendly nor contentious. Red meant that the relationship with the customer had some friction or points of contention. Dealing with these customers was uncomfortable and difficult.

The results of their assessments were then matched to a scatterplot of customer size against the average discount that customer received for the company's flagship product, as shown in Figure 8.1. The grey-shading

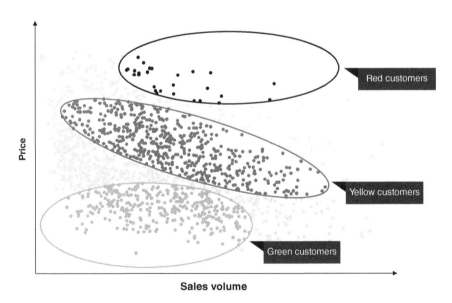

Figure 8.1 What happens when you map the salespeople's view of their customer relationship (red-yellow-green) with customer purchase volumes and prices

shows the contrast between red, yellow, and green (from top to bottom) and each area is labelled.

The red customers in the top oval – the ones perceived as the most difficult – received the lowest discounts, regardless of size. The results for the yellow customers (middle oval) seemed both intuitively and logically correct. There was a correlation between size and discount for the yellow customers, indicating that the company had a system of volume discounts that worked according to plan. These customers received proper attention and salespeople exercised greater care.

The green customers in the bottom oval, however, tended to receive the largest discounts, regardless of size. In the subsequent discussion with the salespeople, it turned out that the green customers were also most likely to be 'service hogs', the kinds of customers that constantly ask for and receive free above-and-beyond support in a wide range of forms. It seemed as if the salespeople were 'buying friendship' by fostering these relationships with ongoing concessions.

The irony is that the 'stoplight' colour scheme describing the relationships corresponded to the traffic signals that the buyers themselves perceived. A 'green' customer had a green light to keep asking for more, safe in the knowledge that the salesperson would honour their requests. 'Yellow' customers played a game of give-and-take. 'Red' customers didn't win concessions, but interestingly, they still bought the product at the relatively high prices.

Why do these green customers receive such large discounts and concessions? Saying 'yes' has become a habit well attuned to one of our evolutionary pre-sets: the desire to be liked. Being liked is a central motivation behind the green relationships. Put another way, when 'yes' is a salesperson's untrained dominant response, saying 'no' to a request for a lower price will make the salesperson uncomfortable. They agree to the discount request to avoid putting their perceived positive relationship at risk.

The innate desire to be liked is the deepest source of the difficulties to say 'no'. From an evolutionary standpoint, it is yet another example of why modern humans are essentially cavepeople in designer clothes. Getting excluded from the community or thrown out of the tribe was a death sentence 10,000 years ago. Being liked played an important role in inclusion and thus to improving our chances of survival. It leads us to hide or suppress anything that could endanger our membership in the tribe.

Anthropologist Clifford Geertz elaborated on this concept in his seminal work *The Interpretation of Cultures*: 'These congruities of blood, speech, custom, and so on, are seen to have an ineffable, and at times overpowering, coerciveness in and of themselves . . . The general strength of such primordial bonds, and the types of them that are important, differ from person to person, from society to society, and from time to time. But for virtually every person, in every society, at almost all times, some attachments seem to flow more from a sense of natural – some would say spiritual – affinity than from social interaction.'[6]

In the spirit of cognitive dissonance, the desire to remain bonded to a group can even be stronger than the belief in the tribe itself. In describing the temple-going behaviours among the Balinese, a culture he studied extensively, Geertz wrote, 'You can believe virtually anything you want to actually, including that the whole thing is rather a bore, and even say so. But if you do not perform the ritual duties for which you are responsible you will be totally ostracized, not just from the temple congregation, but from the community as a whole.'[7]

Within the context of corporate sales negotiation, a salesperson could think that saying 'no' to a discount request would violate a norm and put them at risk of ostracization. The risk of such a fate can make even a twenty-first-century businessperson feel as uncomfortable as a tribe member. Ostracization can range from a temporary denial of access (the customer doesn't return your emails or calls) to exclusion from the customer community. At a time when relationships are vital to a salesperson's success, no one wants to risk being on the outside looking in.

Let's see where we stand so far

Before we show the specific, proven steps you can take to make 'no' your dominant response – and establish a basis for irresistible pricing – let's first recap Part II so far.

- **Prices can cause both pleasure and pain:** They also trigger various emotions that additional stress can intensify. This means that a price decision is always an emotional decision, and not a purely mathematical or logical one. It places demands on System 1 and System 2. In detail, there are several forces in our minds that distort how buyers and sellers assess risks and outcomes. These forces are universal.
- **Discounting is the salesperson's path of least resistance**: The salesperson's natural inclination is to yield to a buyer's request for a concession, especially the request for a lower price or a discount. This reflects what we refer to as their untrained dominant response.
- **Discounts are costly:** The ghost of *homo economicus* still has some truths to tell. The calculations show that when a salesperson grants a discount, it is difficult for a company to break even in terms of revenue, and highly unlikely if not impossible for it to break even in terms of profit.
- **Several forces make it hard to resist the path of least resistance:** One could argue that money is the easiest way for salespeople to make customers happy and maintain a relationship with no extra effort, because it is the easiest customer-facing parameter to change. Cognitive dissonance encourages us to ignore the maths and logic that tells us that discounts harm the company's short-term profits and potentially its long-term value. Prospect theory

describes how we distort the value of our relationships with buyers, and thus how much is at stake. Finally, people have a primordial desire to be liked. The ubiquitous obsession with sales growth intensifies these three effects, in part because it is much easier for salespeople to track their own revenue precisely. In contrast, it takes a team – and often considerable time – to figure out a deal's total profitability.

- **The solution is to change the salesperson's dominant response to 'no':** Discounts are emotional decisions. Limiting or preventing them therefore requires an emotional counterstrategy grounded in science. The naturally confident, consistent dominant response of a salesperson should be 'no' when a buyer asks for a concession.
- **The key, however, is to make 'no' easier, not to make 'yes' harder:** Conventional attempts to change a dominant response involve trying to suppress the untrained dominant response (make the 'yes' harder) rather than to change it by making the 'no' easier. That is why discounts remain commonplace, despite investments in training, incentives, rules, and procedures to discourage or prevent them.

Success in the Invisible Game – and the pricing game within the game – requires behavioural change. Hence, the recommendations in the rest of Part II will equip you with leading-edge self-development tools.

Chapter 9

Expand Your Comfort Zone

For all the talk in negotiations about getting to 'yes,' the word 'no' may be the most valuable word any salesperson will say in the course of a negotiation.[1] This has tactical as well strategic implications. In line with their training, most buyers follow the same general playbook that encourages them to push for more and more concessions – price or otherwise – until they finally hear the salesperson utter the word 'no'. In their playbook, only the seller's 'No!' marks the end of a negotiation.

It would be easy to offer a platitude of 'just say no' as a recommendation, but that would be identical to telling a frightened person to simply stop being afraid. Such suggestions are not practical advice, no matter how well intended they may be. If 'no' seems to cross your lips with conviction, but your body – through sweat, lack of eye contact, a catch in your voice, or any other subtle gesture – betrays you, then you have probably made matters worse, not better.

Changing a dominant response is a journey of self-improvement. In the world of sales negotiation, our narrow focus is to make 'no' your dominant response when a buyer requests a concession, and to ensure that you deliver that 'no' comfortably, confidently, and consistently. The process we describe and explain in this chapter applies to any situation when someone would like to change and then reinforce a new dominant response.

There is a lot of truth to the old saying that the only human being that likes change is a baby with a wet nappy. Change is a challenge for the human brain, which thrives on efficiency through the use of routines. The steps in this chapter aim to help you overcome the challenge of change.

Comfort zones are real

Think of your comfort zone as the sum of behaviours that have worked successfully for you in the past. All those experiences provided System 1 with a ready-to-go menu of ways to recognize and respond to standard situations you come across.

The more frequently we encounter standard situations and respond to them, the more likely our own autopilots are to draw on this narrow but deep set of past experiences.

How many times have we all heard or read 'Leave your comfort zone!' In our view, that appeal for change is hollow and futile for a couple of reasons. First, the sheer thought of leaving one's comfort zone is outright scary for most people. It stokes fear instead of reducing it. But more importantly, the thought of leaving your comfort zone – both semantically and practically – makes no sense as your comfort zone is built upon a wealth of your past positive experiences. And who would want to leave all that behind and walk into uncertainty?

What you can do, however, is use new input to push the boundaries created by those past learnings and prior experiences. Think of your comfort zone as a kind of software package. You update it regularly rather than discarding or replacing it. If salespeople want to stay ahead in a business world full of constant change, it is vitally important for them to expand their comfort zones constantly through new encounters, new situations, and new ideas.

Plan for premieres

You could think of this as seeking 'premieres' in your life, and then following them up with 'encores'. You do something for the first time ever, starting with something seemingly trivial, but then working your way up to more difficult challenges. Then you repeat the process.

You don't need to start with looking for a new job in Brazil, learning Mandarin, or taking an improvisation class with a professional comedy troupe. Look for adjacent activities first before adding new ones. The process can start with taking a new route to work. More advanced steps can include getting involved in different teams at work, from day-to-day business to new initiatives. You can try out new IT applications you have resisted or ignored, or you can place a phone call to customers you may have resisted or ignored because the chemistry seemed off.

The scientific linchpin in this process is a concept called neuroplasticity, which is 'a general umbrella term that refers to the brain's ability to modify, change, and adapt both structure and function throughout life and in response to experience'.[2] The changes in the brain correlate with the types of experiences. In other words, positive changes in the brain generally reflect positive experiences. Ongoing stresses, in contrast, can inhibit positive changes in the brain or lead to negative ones. One relevant part of the brain in this context is the amygdala, which is one of the regions of the brain that governs how we respond to fearful and stressful situations and how we manage our emotions.

Robert Sapolsky describes this in his book *Behave: The Biology of Humans at Our Worst and Best:* 'Sustained stress has numerous adverse effects. The amygdala becomes overactive and more coupled to pathways of habitual behaviour; it is easier to learn fear and harder to unlearn it. We process emotionally salient information more rapidly and automatically, but with less accuracy. Frontal function – working memory, impulse control, executive decision making, risk assessment, and task shifting – is impaired, and the frontal cortex has less control over the amygdala. And we become less empathic and prosocial. Reducing sustained stress is a win-win for us and those stuck around us.'[3]

Repeating your premieres with encores helps you create new routines and expand the pool of experiences that System 1 can draw on. As we said in Part I, the food or fuel for System 1 is exposure and experience.

Practice, exposure, practice

Many professionals such as soldiers, athletes, and emergency responders regularly train the intense dominant responses that make them successful in their fields. Their System 1 has been changed permanently, because time and repetition have trained their personal autopilots. System 2 controls whether someone *can* save a person's life, in terms of understanding the necessity and knowing what steps to take. System 1 controls whether they actually *will* save a person's life.

The emphasis on active practice and on pre-programming their automated behaviours is particularly important for salespeople, because they tend to get much less 'real-life' exposure than buyers do. The average industrial buyer has more suppliers to manage than the average salesperson has customers. This gives buyers more exposure to a greater range of products, arguments, personalities, and reference points. As a result, they have more opportunities to expand their comfort zone naturally in the course of day-to-day business.

Salespeople need to try to replicate this breadth and depth by intentionally and purposefully seeking exposure to new experiences. Similar to physical strength training, autopiloted behaviours require active training, so that you can form a highly adaptable personal comfort zone that allows you to respond to any new challenge with agility.

How to make 'No!' your dominant response

The more we hear ourselves say 'no' in different situations, the less stressful that act becomes and the less sensitive we become to both the act (saying 'no') and its feared consequences, such as being disliked or ostracized.

To expand your comfort zone, think of comfort – the obvious antidote to discomfort – in terms of three dimensions:

- The number of stresses – defined as situations, patterns, conflicts, or outcomes – you have exposed yourself to.
- The number of contexts in which you are exposed to for each source of stress.
- The number of times you are exposed to them.

The more you can expose yourself to a particular source of stress, especially in different contexts, the more you can instil a better – and more powerful – dominant response. In short, you can't say 'no' in a stressful situation if you have never said 'no' in a similar situation, or at least in one that your System 1 will view as similar.

John Bargh, a social psychologist from Yale University, refers to the human autopilot as 'automated will' and wrote: 'To shift the regulation of goal pursuit from conscious control to automatic control can be an adaptive way of ensuring goal pursuit, even under new, complex, or difficult circumstances.'[4]

Can salespeople cultivate the kind of automatic control or automated will that Bargh referred to? Gaby is living proof that they can. As a long-time professional B2B salesperson, she knows the temptations of the inner voice very well, the one that wants to say 'yes' and get the deal done. To change her dominant response, she needed to find an easier way to say 'no' instead of sticking with the conventional solutions designed to make 'yes' harder. The breakthroughs for her came from several sources, including a methodology called ZRM (Zuercher Ressourcen Modell, or Zurich Resource Model), which was developed by self-management trainers Maja Storch and Frank Krause of the University of Zurich.

ZRM and similar approaches have worked very well at changing behaviours in many other areas where stress levels are high and where self-management can lead to significant improvement. For example, several studies have demonstrated that these techniques can help people manage eating disorders more effectively and generally do a better job of managing (lowering) levels of the stress hormone cortisol.[5,6] Another meta-study concluded that, '[g]oal-setting based intervention appeared to improve symptom control, quality of life and self-efficacy in adult patients with asthma.'[7]

We believe this publication marks the first time someone has applied these approaches to changing behaviours in professional sales situations. The three steps in Figure 9.1 represent a well-grounded fusion of science and practice.

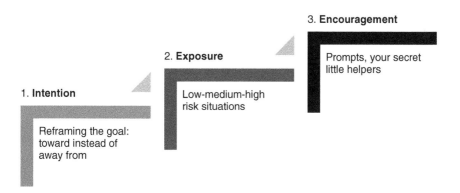

Figure 9.1 The three steps to expanding your comfort zone and making changes to your dominant responses

Step 1: Intention keeps you looking forward, not backward

It is tempting to formulate a goal as a rejection of a previous mode of behaviour. We are all familiar with typical examples, such as: 'I will no longer be afraid of that situation' or 'I want to lose weight.' Even detailed goals take on that form, such as: 'I will not stress-eat when work gets tough.' A similar phrasing for a salesperson would be: 'I will not give in the next time they ask for a lower price.'

Each of those statements has one thing in common. They all have a double-negative construction, with the undesired state combined with another negative word like 'not' or 'lose'. That is a lot of negativity!

The ZRM approach recommends that you frame goals in a positive way. The difference is a matter of science, not merely semantics. You resolve to move toward a new behaviour rather than away from a previous behaviour. In the context of changing the dominant response, it means visualizing the goal positively and affirmatively ('I want to look fit' or 'I will say "no"') rather than placing a negative focus on the old behaviour ('I will not give in').

One rationale for using positive language to express the goal is the effect that negative language has on achievement. A study by two Canadian researchers revealed that 'negative goal framing predicted poorer future performance independent of goal level, expectancy, and earlier performance.'[8] In other words, framing your goal in negative terms directly affects your chances of achieving it. The negative formulation is also open-ended, because it begs the 'how?' question. What behaviour or actions will you undertake to avoid giving in? Positive framing is more specific, and that works well with System 1, which responds more readily to clear, positive direction.

Positive formulations are not only unambiguous. They also change how you measure progress and success. The metric for measuring progress is not defined by the distance from the positioning you are leaving, but rather in terms of the remaining progress you need to reach your goal.

Step 2: Exposure means practising in a structured, progressive way

To provide structure and a clear path to progress, the ZRM method defines A, B, and C situations for practising the new intentional behaviours you want to programme. To avoid confusion with business uses of A-B-C, such as for customer segmentations, we will describe these situations instead as low risk, medium risk, and high risk.

In Figure 9.2 we look at the Dominant Response Matrix again, but from the perspective of your personal challenges and their impact on you personally. What are some events or situations that you would imagine taking place in the lower left?

These *low-risk situations* are simple, low stress, and low stakes opportunities for you to practise a new intentional behaviour, such as the act of saying 'no'. One common low-risk situation for many people is routine shopping. The next time you go to a new shop and the person at the counter asks you to join their loyalty programme or sign up for their store credit card, you decline – with a clear 'No, thank you.' It is important that you hear yourself utter the word and offer no embellishment, excuses, or apologies for your 'No!' The 'no' needs to stand on its own, without qualification.

Medium-risk situations warrant more preparation because they should take place in a business context rather than a private one. In the Dominant Response Matrix, these situations are in the middle band, where the stress, scrutiny, complexity, and/or impact have increased. Offer a 'no' in a somewhat more complex situation, but where the stakes are still not overwhelming or threatening. Then allow your System 2 to take over and view the issue at hand logically, critically, and systematically. You may find yourself declining a customer request in an area not directly related to price. You

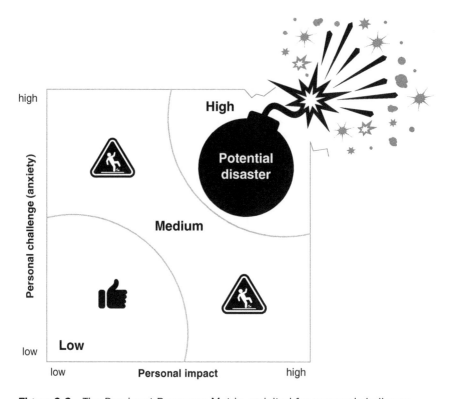

Figure 9.2 The Dominant Response Matrix, revisited for personal challenge and impact

might turn down a request for special services, shorter delivery time, additional free samples, or the waiving of delivery fees or other surcharges.

Social facilitation can also play a role here. Recall from the cockroach study that if a crowd watches you do a simple, habitual, or routine task, the chances are that you will perform better than if you did the task in isolation.

This means that as you advance, you should let people observe you in the act of saying 'no' in an effort to reinforce the new dominant response. Letting others observe you saying 'no' also starts to establish a new sense of accountability. A study from Dominion University in California concluded that accountability – in the form of sharing goals and progress with others – correlated with better success in goal achievement.[9] A meta-study published in the bulletin of the American Psychological Association came to a similar conclusion. It noted that, 'progress monitoring had larger effects on goal attainment when the outcomes were reported or made public, and when the information was physically recorded. Taken together, the findings suggest that monitoring goal progress is an effective self-regulation strategy, and that interventions that increase the frequency of progress monitoring are likely to promote behavior change.'[10]

High-risk situations are masterclass situations, the hardest ones to tackle. They represent high stress and high stakes. Often, just thinking about them makes you sweat. They could also represent business situations where you have fallen short of success. Within the Dominant Response Matrix, such situations would be in the upper outer band.

These situations require special thought and preparation. Remember to avoid negativity in your goal setting. It is your journey towards a new behaviour, not getting away from what might have happened in the past. Set a new positive and affirmative goal for yourself to decline a customer request that you have previously considered difficult to decline. This could be a pricing concession or any other unwarranted demand. Think of a specific customer and their typical request. Visualize the situation and make a conscious decision that the next time that the customer asks you for a concession, your answer will be 'no, we cannot do that' together with no more than three reasons. Offering these reasons together with the 'no' is an important step toward one of the objectives we laid out in Part I, namely, that the ideal mode of operation for a salesperson is the optimal combination of System 1 and System 2.

Once you have a specific situation identified, it is very important to note your intended new behaviour as succinctly and unequivocally as possible: 'When/if the customer asks for. . . ., I will reply with. . . .' Such prepared statements – examples of System 1 and System 2 working together – are important, because you can access them in high-stress situations.

Success rates in high-risk situations will not be 100%. But each 'no' means progress in expanding your comfort zone.

Step 3: Use prompts and other aids for encouragement

People often desire to follow through with their plans, yet frequently fail to do so. Some of these plans are singular and ambitious, such as reaching a goal weight. Others have more regular rhythms, such as conducting overdue business calls when driving to work or changing the air filter in the kitchen hood every six months.

An electronic reminder can be very effective for some of these tasks. But electronic devices do not sense the moment in a Zoom call when your pulse goes up, you experience enhanced microsweating, and your old dominant responses risk steering you back to old behavioural patterns.

To find ways for people to overcome these chronic follow-through failures, Harvard's Todd Rogers and Wharton's Katy Milkman conducted a study in which they ran six experiments: some online and some offline.[11] They tested various reminders and discovered that prompts help participants remember a specific task when those prompts, or reminders, are particularly distinctive.

In one experiment, they handed out a discount voucher to each visitor to a coffee shop. As many of us have experienced, people often forget to redeem these vouchers and get frustrated. What can improve redemption?

Half of the visitors in the experiment received a plain paper voucher, while the other half received the same voucher but with a picture of stuffed toy alien and the additional reference: 'To remind you Thursday, this will be on the cash register.'

The stuffed toy alien that appeared at the cash register on Thursday served as an effective prompt. More visitors who received the alien on their voucher redeemed their coupons than those who received the voucher with no image. Rogers and Milkman's other five experiments, all making a similar point, allowed them to present a strong case for the use of distinctive prompts. Independently, an elaborate brain scan study established that graspable items in a person's lower right visual field attract particular attention.[12]

Based on that study and the insights from Rogers and Milkman, it makes sense for people to choose small tangible items as distinctive reminders or prompts to repeat and reinforce a certain behaviour. In practice, this means you can set up your own prompts for the Invisible Game, such as a little toy anchor next to your phone.

The ZRM approach recommends such prompts. Specifically, the approach suggests that people 'systematically set up and equip their environments with reminders to ensure that the new neural pathway is always activated, even when their attention is caught up in other matters'.[13] This means that such objects can have the desired effect even when the causal link is not consciously perceived.[14]

Prompts are personal and private. Unless you let someone in on the secret, no one else knows that a particular object or image serves as your prompt. You have free latitude to select the object or image that will embody a learned association for you. Think of the object as a 'mental fuelling station.' In online meetings, it is easy to place these prompts within your line of sight. You can set them on the desk or wall behind your computer, outside the visual field of the participants onscreen. At other meeting occasions, you could choose an object that is already in the conference room, such as a chair or a flip chart, or you bring a special pen that you associate with your new intended behaviour. In each case, you choose a prompt according to your personal preferences.

At some point the behaviour that you are trying to reinforce – in this case, saying 'no' in a negotiation – becomes a dominant response that works independently of the presence of the prompt. When that time comes, you need to let go of that specific prompt and not use that object again. Developing the next new behaviour requires a completely different object. In other words, you can't recycle a prompt.

In the final chapter of Part II, we will explore some of the common tactics that buyers have in their playbook. They can use them to heighten the stress level in a negotiation artificially in an effort to trigger a response that works to the salesperson's detriment.

Chapter 10

From the Buyer's Playbook: Time, Uncertainty, Fear, and Silence

The context of a negotiation exists independently of the actors. Framing is how each actor tries to influence that context. By placing emphasis on certain aspects and setting the priorities, the framer establishes how each actor understands the context. The framer also imposes limits on their leeway to operate within it. These frames can range from classical nudges to a complete rewriting of the rules or reshaping of the playing field.

Buyers use several techniques – such as time, uncertainty, fear, and silence – to ensure that negotiations take place on their home field with their ground rules. In some cases, they will try to rewrite those ground rules by reframing the entire negotiation. Part II concludes with a peek into the buyer's playbook to show you how these techniques work and how you can withstand them and neutralize their advantages. Sellers need to reject these frames and, if possible, attempt to impose their own.

How buyers play with time and timing

Time can be an especially dangerous influence. Buyers gain a considerable advantage by controlling it: deadlines, meeting length, start and end times, for example. People tend to underestimate the extent to which time messes not only with our heads but can even shake our core beliefs.

Let's take a brief timeout for a quiz. Imagine that someone is in a small city for a meeting and is rushing to get to the destination, because they are late for a meeting. Along the way, they pass by a person who obviously needs assistance. How likely is that person to stop and offer help?

a. 1%
b. 10%
c. 25%
d. 40%

Most people are familiar with the phrase 'Good Samaritan', which describes a person who goes out of their way to offer help to a stranger in distress. That original story about the Good Samaritan takes up a mere 200 words in the Gospel of Luke, but over centuries it has come to define a desirable code of behaviour that most people aspire to emulate.[1]

How applicable is that story to the hectic pressures of modern life? That question prompted two professors at Princeton University to conduct an experiment. They wanted to find out how many people would act as Good Samaritans if they were in a hurry. The participants in the experiments were all scheduled to give a presentation in a nearby building. The professors exposed them to one of three situations: high hurry ('you're already late'), intermediate hurry ('they are ready for you; you should get going'), and low hurry ('they will be ready soon; you should get going'). Along the way, each participant encountered the proverbial stranger in distress.

Before we compare your quiz answer to the findings of the Princeton researchers, let's add to additional assumptions to the quiz. What if the people in our quiz question were all seminary students, training for the priesthood? What if the presentation they were scheduled to give was a sermon about being a Good Samaritan? Under these assumptions, how would you revise your answer?

The reason we added those assumptions is because they represent the conditions the Princeton team tested. The participants in the survey were seminary students, and the findings from the experiment demonstrate clearly how artificially manipulated triggers can lead people to act in ways that conflict with or even violate what they profess as core values. Some 63% of the 'low hurry' seminary students did indeed stop to help the victim. In the case of the 'intermediate-hurry' scenario, 45% of the participants helped, but in the 'high-hurry' case – the one in which the students were late for their sermon – only 10% stopped to act as a Good Samaritan. This held true regardless of whether the topic of the sermon was about the Good Samaritan or a sermon on giving and helping in general.[2]

The moral of this Good Samaritan experiment is that time pressure messes with our heads and our beliefs. These effects occur in sales negotiations as well. Witness what transpires within the span of 30 minutes in this following true story about a sales team on its way to meet a key account.

It is 9:50 a.m. outside a gleaming office building in a major city centre., Josie is sitting with her team colleagues in the reception area at Shielding Inc.[3] She has already checked in for the 10:00 a.m. meeting with Anton Smith, the head of purchasing. Josie and her team are not only positive and full of energy, but also well prepared for the day. Today's meeting concerns the renewal of a large supply contract for a third year. Her company has already won this contract twice in previous years against its competitors and is banking on the $10 million in revenue that the renewal would bring in. Josie and her team have to strike a deal today.

Now the clock says 10:05 a.m. They are still waiting in the reception area.

Josie asks at the reception desk whether she has perhaps missed a step in the check-in process. They reassure her that everything is ok. Slowly the tension rises. She and her colleagues look at each other quizzically, trying to understand why the purchasing team is keeping them waiting. Perhaps a small crisis has suddenly come up? Maybe they want them to wait to sap their energy or psych them out? Maybe it is simply for the sake of waiting? They have no idea what is going on and stare with increasing nervousness at the clock in the reception area: 10:10, 10:11, 10:12 . . . 10:15.

At 10:20, Josie writes a WhatsApp message to Mr Smith:

Good morning, Anton. I assume that something unforeseen has occurred to prevent you from taking our meeting today. I'm sorry about that. We don't want to impose any additional burden on you and will now leave for the day. I will contact you again tomorrow to schedule a new meeting.

Two minutes later, the phone rings at the reception desk. Josie and her team are asked to wait, because Mr Smith will meet them momentarily. Three more minutes go by before Mr Smith exits the elevator, together with Schielding Inc.'s managing director. They apologize profusely for the delay, citing the need to take an unanticipated call from the CEO. Josie recognizes that excuse as one of the oldest and weakest excuses that a purchaser might give, but she tries to suppress and disguise her disbelief. She smiles and accepts the apology. Both parties head upstairs to begin the meeting.

The steps taken by both parties between 9:50 a.m. and 10:20 a.m. reflect a battle for power and control. Smith's side made an attempt to subordinate and intimidate Josie's party through their actions. They had their attempt immediately countered by a veiled threat from Josie, whose team could now enter the negotiation without a sudden and adverse shift in the balance of power.

Josie has trained herself to recognize the signal of such power play and resist the urge to give in. The urge to accept the other side's actions stems from the human desire to be liked, which we discussed in Chapter 8. She had trained her System 1 to ignore the urge to please by expanding the boundaries of her comfort zone. That's why she could confront such situation with a clear 'No! Not acceptable!'

Would Josie have left if that call hadn't come through to the reception? Absolutely she would have! Over the years, she had learned not to make idle threats, which means she had every intention to follow through. She knows that it is always important to make it clear that your time is just as valuable as your business partner's time.

Time is a powerful offensive and defensive weapon, precisely because it is a scarce resource. People can use timeouts to process information and engage or recharge System 2, and people can use artificial stress and time pressure to force another party to respond in ways that work against that party's interests.

Be aware that time is also a powerful tactic to drive decision making. The extent of the advantages and disadvantages depends on who controls time and timings. Think back to the study with the cockroaches. What happens to our dominant response when someone imposes artificial stress on an otherwise easy situation? The key word in that sentence is artificial. Many of the constraints that people perceive – both in their personal and professional lives – lead them to veer away from the desired and proper form of response that they would have if the constraint were not present. People can develop phobias when they face continued exposure to artificial conditions. Professional buyers know this and take advantage of it systematically.

To dive deeper into the psychological and physiological effects of time, let us pose a situation. Assume that you have to make a short speech. You have two options. Either you can speak for two minutes, or you can speak until a slice of bread pops from a toaster. Which option would you choose?

Our speculation is that you would select the option of two minutes, because it provides certainty and it allows you to plan your talk better than when you cannot anticipate the end. We also assume that you would opt for the two minutes even though one study has shown that the ideal timespan for toasting a slice of bread is 216 seconds (or 3 minutes, 36 seconds) which would allow you much more time to speak.[4]

To say that our minds don't like uncertainty, however, is an oversimplification. What bothers us – mentally and physically – is anticipation, or more precisely, an artificial gap or delay between the expected timing of an event and its actual occurrence. This is the flip side of the power of timeouts. In Part I we mentioned that sports teams use timeouts as an opportunity to rest, rethink, and regroup. But sports teams also tap into this power when they call a timeout late in a game in order to 'ice the shooter' before a basketball free throw or 'ice the kicker' before a decisive field goal attempt in football. Buyers do something similar when they ask a sales team to sit in the lobby or wait outside beyond the scheduled start of a meeting. The common interpretation is that this is a 'psychological tactic' on the buyers' part. But this is an insufficient explanation, because it offers neither a precise 'why' nor the basis for a solution. Why do people use the tactic, and why is it still effective in many cases even when the intended target often knows that the other side might deploy it?

The untrained mind's response in such a situation is that one's imagination that starts to run wild and attribute the delay to any number of causes. What could the problem be? Are we on shaky ground?

Think of it this way: 'It's like when the lights go out and you feel something behind you. You hear it, you feel its breath against your ear, but when you turn around, there's nothing there.' Even if there is no 'there' there, the longer we wait, the more we start speculating: what is going on?

That is how the novelist Stephen King defines terror.[5]

How buyers play with uncertainty and fear

System 1 hates uncertainty and wants consistency and stability. That need is especially strong when urgency or fear plays a role. The greater the perceived urgency of a situation, or the greater the level of uncertainty and fear involved, the more people will rely on System 1 for a decision and ignore System 2. These decisions are generally known as a 'fight or flight,' a visceral reaction driven by System 1. It is our primitive mechanism for self-preservation and remains an active and strong force in all humans to this day.

One difficulty with 'fight or flight' is that our System 1 has not evolved sufficiently to keep up with the modern life that thrives on System 2. The chances are almost negligible that today's cavepeople wearing designer suits will die directly from the activities they conduct in their fancy offices. But uncertainty still causes the fear of a severe loss. This alarm even creeps into salespeople's language, articulated in thoughts such as *'if we lose this deal, we are toast'* or *'losing this deal could kill my business'*. System 1 kicks into overdrive in order to prevent this metaphorical death, not a real one.

Fear is the worst partner you can imagine. Addressing that core fear of losing the deal is important because many of the other fears derive from it. It infiltrates your mind and influences your behaviour. If you are afraid of not getting the business, you can start to fear for your ability to meet a target and to earn a bonus that was going to pay a tuition bill, fund a surprise vacation, or get you that new SUV. In its worst case, you may even fear for your livelihood.

Of course, buyers know this. When they undergo their own negotiation trainings, they hear one simple sentence, over and over, until it becomes second nature for them: the salesperson's greatest fear is losing the deal. The purchasers know that they can turn up the intensity in a negotiation by making that statement explicit rather than implicit, especially in highly competitive industries where there is not much differentiation among suppliers.

Why would the buyers do that? They know that they can use fear as a weapon. That one ominous sentence about losing the deal has such a powerful psychological as well as a physiological impact on the salesperson. It momentarily paralyzes them, then creates an opportunity for the buyer to reframe the negotiation. At that moment, they know that the salesperson becomes more susceptible to the repetition of short messages because they will trigger a System 1 response. When that happens to you – and it will – what will your response be?

If your response to conquer the fear and reduce uncertainty is to cling to stability, then you are more likely to put yourself into a smaller box and colour between the lines. You will attempt to play it safe, and you will be more likely to acquiesce to what the purchaser wants. When buyers re-define the frame for the negotiation, they force the salespeople to believe in reinforced stereotypes as they try to adjust to the new frame.

But if your response from System 1 is more nuanced and better informed by a range of past experiences and pre-programming, you might be able to recognize the new frame for what it is: the buyer's attempt to stoke fears and capitalize on the stresses of the negotiation. This recognition helps you resist the new frame.

How buyers play with silence

The absence of literal communication is a powerful form of communication, as Gaby can attest. She had a very close relationship with the head of purchasing at one of the largest companies in a portfolio she once managed. She was about the same age as Gaby and was always friendly. She reached out almost daily, not only to align on current business topics, but also to have a casual personal chat.

But then one day, she temporarily cut off communication after Gaby said 'no' to a discount request. For almost a month, she neither called nor responded to Gaby's calls. When she finally did resume contact, she never mentioned the incident which – in Gaby's mind – had precipitated the silent treatment.

Gaby had felt the same emotions that one would feel in a family quarrel, when someone gets the cold shoulder for a minor offence that eventually blows over. It taught her that silence is another powerful weapon that makes people uncomfortable. As Gaby managed her withdrawal symptoms during the silent period, she observed herself fighting back the urge to send a mail saying 'Sorry, of course you get the discount!' and thus atone for her supposed wrongdoing.

Most salespeople have a similar story to tell. This is another form of framing in the Invisible Game, and salespeople need to recognize it and exert self-control. Sometimes the secret to winning lies in steeling yourself to endure the silence, resist the urge to act, and wait for the other person to get back to you. Otherwise you teach your customer that silence is a sure way to manipulate you (see Situation 10.1).

If you change your offer in the absence of such information, you risk losing face or losing your credibility. Be sceptical about yourself when you get anxious waiting for a reply. Instead of jumping to conclusions, you might be able to call a trusted source in your customer's company and have a friendly chat about another topic. This may put your mind at ease and even draw out some information on why you haven't received a response.

Situation 10.1: No news is bad news. I've blown this deal!

I sent an offer to a key account last week, and if they accept, I'll be close to achieving my sales bonus this year. What have I heard so far? Crickets. It's been days, and now I'm on pins and needles. I'm counting hours and the minutes as I constantly refresh my inbox.

Why hasn't the client called me back? What did I do wrong? Was my letter not up to their expectation? Was my price too high? Should I send a mail to my contact saying that the pricing is still negotiable?

It was hard on my nerves, but luckily, I refrained from sending such a mail. Today – one week after I sent the offer – my key account accepted. They also apologized for the delay. My counterpart on their team was sick and out of the office for a week.

What is the science behind this? The effect is called the fundamental attribution error. It appears in many forms and on many occasions, compelling us to take action when we should instead be waiting for another party to respond. The fundamental attribution error leads people to underestimate the importance and nature of the current situation, while overestimating the importance of stable underlying issues. As a result, people speculate wildly about why something is happening, when the actual reasons and causes are almost always far simpler, less dramatic, and a result of temporary circumstances.

People also might attribute undesirable outcomes to their own behaviour or personality rather than to the circumstances. It explains why people have a tendency to believe that everyone is watching them or that their role or influence is greater than it actually is.

What is our recommendation? Sit tight, wait, and look for real underlying causes. As a rule of thumb, the non-reply is situational and has nothing to do with you personally in 99% of all cases. We take it as a given that you did your homework in advance and constructed your offer properly based on your customer and competitive intelligence. Unless you receive new information that changes the context of your offer, it stands. Period.

A moment of silence is also a very powerful technique in any business situation, especially when you want more information, or the time has come for the other party to make a decision. Most people we know have a hard time with moments of silence during a conversation. They feel the urge to fill the silence, which loosens their tongue and risks that they will share more that they should. Try a moment of silence. When you have an opportunity, smile at the other party and remain silent for about 10 to 15 seconds. You'll be surprised what gets revealed.

How buyers rewrite the rules or change the playing field

Imagine that you work for an ingredients company called Xevono. You hear through industry channels that a company called Starlight is about to acquire one of your important customers, Peter & Friends, a start-up successful in marketing cosmetic products to male consumers.[6] Starlight is a much larger organization that sells a broad range of personal care products through its own outlets, and the specialty lines from Peter & Friends are an ideal fit for the popular Starlight shelves.

Xevono helped Peter & Friends develop and implement their original marketing and sales strategy, creating a mutually beneficial relationship that rapidly accelerated Xevono's profitable growth. But Xevono has so far never been able to develop a fruitful sales relationship with Starlight. This acquisition therefore opens up an opportunity for more sales growth if Starlight is impressed with the excellent service performance you have delivered to Peter & Friends.

Then just as quickly as that window opens, it threatens to slam shut on your fingers. Shortly after the acquisition became public, an email from Starlight appears in your inbox. It's a form letter from their purchasing department, communicating its two prerequisites for continuing your business relationship with what is now a larger organization with more marketing and buying power. They want an immediate 25% onboarding discount and an extension of their payment terms to 150 days.

As you read those details this story, what did you think right away? How should respond to the demands?

Such emails are common. Many other suppliers around the world have received similar ultimatum letters that contain the kinds of egregious conditions that Starlight wants to impose. This situation occurs in every industry and every region. Right now, those suppliers are also scratching their heads, just as you are, in an effort to find the right answer for their particular situation.

Let's boil your possible responses down to two options, each of which is in the spirit of what you just absorbed in Part II.

1. **Say 'no' in clear, unequivocal terms:** You write back to Starlight and state that your calculations do not allow discounts of that magnitude, and that payment terms of 150 days are a non-starter because of the obvious detrimental effects on cash flow.
2. **Imply 'no' by asking Starlight for a meeting:** You write back to invite Starlight's purchasing team to a meeting to discuss the 25% discount and 150 days. Your objective – left unstated in your response – is to negotiate them down to something more reasonable.

If you go with the first option, Part II should have prepared you to deliver that response with confidence. After all, if any request for a discount deserves a forceful rejection, it is Starlight's. The second option offers several potential advantages. It will leave the Starlight purchasing team with some uncertainty. It will buy you time for more thorough analyses to prepare your precise counteroffers. Finally, it will add to the context that will help you infer how serious their offer is and then calibrate your response. Right now, their aggressive demands are their opening moves in the attempt to frame the Visible Game and the Invisible Game.

Nonetheless . . . it might surprise you that we recommend neither of these options.

Part II showed you how to say 'no' to a specific request from a customer during a negotiation. In Part III, we explore how to say 'no' to the *entire context* of a negotiation, and then establish your own frames. That is the best response to Starlight's email.

The motivation behind emails such as Starlight's is to establish a new set of anchors and redraw the frame of the negotiation. If you choose either Option 1 or Option 2, you have swallowed the bait. You have tacitly agreed to their negotiating context, even though you have rejected the proposal or implied that you will make a counteroffer. Regardless of what ultimately happens with the numbers, you will have negotiated within rules unilaterally set by Starlight and with anchors that Starlight set.

What should you do instead? The moves we describe in the following list weave together many of the insights we have presented so far, from situational awareness to anchoring to confidence and control.

- **Limit exposure to Starlight's email:** What will happen if you share that email internally, so that the rest of the team can share your indignation at Starlight's audacity and unfairness? Suddenly you will hear the numbers 25 and 150 come up in conversations, and that is precisely what Starlight would want. Anchors are sticky numbers. Sending that email around ensures that those two numbers remain at the forefront of everyone's thinking. So don't do Starlight's work by letting their anchors go viral within your team, in the true infectious (and negative) sense of that word.
- **Engage your situational awareness:** You should recognize the letter for what it is: an attempt to influence the buying decision in Starlight's favour. Register the attempt and ignore the numbers as best as you can. These emails not only deliver anchors, but also aim to elicit a response that will allow the sender to infer how much leverage they have, how unsettled the sellers are, and how they can take advantage of the pending negotiations.
- **Respond in kind, but do not acknowledge their numbers:** One forceful way to say 'no' to the context is to counter immediately with your own anchor. You could send them a letter congratulating them on the acquisition of Peter & Friends, thank them for their interest in your products, and suggest a meeting to discuss business continuation. But in contrast to Option 2 above, your response must never

acknowledge that you have received or seen any numbers, never mind what the numbers are or that you cannot afford them. Some companies have gone a step further in their response letters by announcing price increases (for example, up to 15%) to set a new anchor.

These steps belong to a more advanced version of the Invisible Game. They allow a seller to find a way to say 'no' without actually explicitly saying 'no' or even acknowledging that there was a question in the first place. The seller aims instead to create their own new frame for the working relationship with Starlight and Peter & Friends, including new price anchors.

What we have learned in Part II

In Part II we have shown how to develop a stronger mental core that will empower you to say 'no' to a discount or any other concession request. But getting to that point required a thorough exploration of the emotional side of a sales negotiation.

That starts with the emotional and sensory power that prices exert on both buyers and sellers. Prices are where the lines between the Visible Game and the Invisible Game blur. Most salespeople are unaware that buyers have a maximum feel-good price in their minds that usually lies well above the prices explicitly discussed between the parties. Buyers work hard to keep it that way by affecting the frame of the negotiation, keeping the stress level for sellers high, and pushing for discounts.

Sellers overcome their fear of 'no' by understanding the reasons behind that fear, and then expanding their comfort zones by redefining their goals, gaining new experiences in a structured way, and using prompts to reinforce their progress.

Part III

Playing Offence and the Powers of Influence

S ales outperformers don't win only because they play the Invisible Game well. They win because they determine how the Invisible Game will be played. They establish and enforce frames in a sales situation by defining the decision criteria, the range of outcomes, the degrees of freedom, and how risks are shared. It's the difference between being the dealer and accepting the hand you are dealt.

In that spirit, Part III shifts the emphasis from defence to offence. It will show salespeople how to establish and preserve a home-field advantage rather than always playing defence in the purchaser's home park with their ground rules and all the other measures of control they can impose. Who can claim home-field advantage often depends on the balance of power in the sales relationship. In Part III, we view that balance as a function of personal and paper power.

At the same time, let's remember that buyers, like sellers and everyone else, are also cavepeople in designer clothes. They have their own pronounced biases that affect how they view their suppliers, how they make decisions, how they perceive gains and losses, and how they respond to price changes. The second half of Part III describes powerful approaches that salespeople can use to frame the negotiation – and the options the buyers have – in ways that work to the seller's advantage.

That is the essence of playing offence in the Invisible Game.

Chapter 11

Personal Versus Paper Power: Where's Your Leverage?

T here is an old sports cliché that underdogs cite after they have beaten a team considered to be superior: 'That's why we play the games.'[1] That cliché also explains why we draw a distinction between personal power and paper power. Paper power – the measure of strength in the Visible Game – relies on tangible factors and arguments that aim to determine which party enjoys an objective advantage. Personal power reflects strength in the Invisible Game. It relies on intangible factors, such as one's ability to influence decision making through frames, choice architectures, and other techniques.

The potential for an uneven balance between personal power and paper power is why sales negotiations still take place. If personal power played no role in a negotiation, then all buying decisions would come down entirely to fact sheets, Excel models, and powerful algorithms. Those objective tools may indicate which competitor is superior and should win the negotiation. But think back to the sales negotiation that Gaby described in the very first story in this book. On paper, Mr Anderson's company should have won that deal. But when the negotiations finished, the underdog Gaby was the one departing New York City with a deal in her briefcase.

Personal power is often potent enough to offset objective advantages that the buyer or another competitor may have. Shifting the balance of personal power in your favour can become the decisive success factor in an intensely competitive market, because it enables you to overcome the advantages conferred by paper power. The balance of personal power is especially important when the differences between any competing offers are slight.

But how do you enhance your personal power so that you can overcome the advantages conferred by paper power? It starts with the ability to assess the balance of personal power before a negotiation and then re-assess it during the negotiation. This often proves difficult, because no party has enough hard information about the other side to make an objective assessment of personal power. The determination, therefore, must derive from situational awareness and from the continuous process of establishing and then validating assumptions. Greater personal power gives a party the leeway to define the frames in a negotiation as well as the terms and the parameters of power in their favour.

One reason why it is vital to assess your balance of power as reliably as possible and project that power effectively is that the buyers are trying to do the same thing. They have the same fears as sellers and are subject to the same illusions and biases. Nobody wants to feel powerless, nor does anyone want the uncertainty of being subject to someone else's whims and decisions. The party who exercises more power controls the path to a decision.

Most suppliers have a customer segmentation, but many fail to realize that their customers have their own supplier segmentations, too. The classic approach that buyers use to determine the overall balance of power between themselves and their suppliers is a segmentation matrix based on an A-B-C analysis and the well-known Pareto rule, along the lines of what is shown in Figure 11.1. This technique has evolved to become a standard approach in the professional buyer's repertoire since a manager from General Electric introduced it 70 years ago.[2] For a typical company, around 20% of suppliers account for 80% of their purchasing spend. Around 15% of total spend is classified as medium-risk and the remaining 5% is usually called the tail. For personal power to matter, it is critical for a supplier or seller to be in that top 20% and have a high impact on the buyer's business.

In Figure 11.1, the importance of a supplier is a function of two factors: volume, which one could objectively measure, and impact on the buyer's

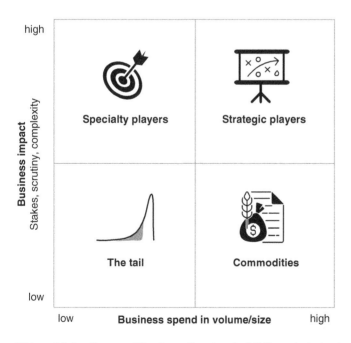

Figure 11.1 Buyers still rely on the classic A-B-C analysis to decide which suppliers receive the most attention and a larger share of a very scarce resource: their time. The most relevant 'A' suppliers are in the buyer's top 20%

business, which is more subjective but something that one could estimate with some accuracy.

The strategic 'A' suppliers land in the upper-right quadrant, because they deliver large volumes, have significant impact on the buyer's business, and would be hard to replace because of their specific know-how. The 'A' suppliers in the lower-right quadrant still deliver large volumes, but with less overall impact on the buyer's business. They are easier to replace. They might not supply commodities in the purest sense of the term, but the loss or replacement of one of these suppliers would generally not put operations at risk. In such cases, it is difficult if not impossible for personal power to offset paper power.

The 'B' suppliers from the upper-left quadrant tend to be smaller versions of the upper-right quadrant 'A' suppliers. The 'C' suppliers in the lower left typically represent the tail, the large number of small suppliers to be managed with a high level of standardization and little investment of attention or time.

This conventional approach focuses on the present and the recent past. Joseph M. Juran, said to be the first person to apply the 80/20 Pareto rule in a managerial context, once described the role of A-B-C analysis by saying that a company has to distinguish between the 'vital few' and the 'trivial many' in order to determine how to allocate their time and attention.[3]

This makes time allocation a valuable indicator for sellers to observe and track. Buyers will try to spend the most time with suppliers that have the highest relevance to their current portfolio. When the risks of making a major mistake are at their lowest – whether in terms of money or quality – buyers will deny time to suppliers and increasingly expose them to transactional 'take-it-or-leave-it' behaviours. In some companies, buyers many even outsource such decisions to automated tools.

How customer transformations are changing the balance of power

Analyses such as the conventional A-B-C segmentation played a vital role in the Old Economy, when decisions depended on factors – such as sales volume – that someone could easily measure or estimate. But there is a massive shift underway in the New Economy. Buyers are focusing their attention equally on their suppliers' current and future capabilities. They still care about the question 'What can you do for me right now?' but are replacing 'What have you done for me lately?' with the question 'What can you do for me – and with me – tomorrow?' The reason is that most companies – and most of your customers – are undergoing significant transformations. Change is everybody's constant, not only yours.

In today's world, no buyer can afford to put their company's future at risk. High-end innovation capabilities are the new Holy Grail for buyers, whose companies are under pressure to introduce their own new products and new models. Buyers are now enhancing their analyses by evaluating their suppliers for their transformation capabilities. Suppliers that are critical to the future success will receive red-carpet treatment.

Figure 11.2 shows how the classic buyer's segmentation matrix changes for companies that are on a journey of transformation.

Your customer strategy, including your pricing, should reflect your status as a supplier. The path to becoming a strategic supplier involves more than high volumes for products with few or no substitutes. To land in the buyer's upper-right quadrant in Figure 11.2 and stay there, a supplier needs to sell their own company's transformation journey and future innovation capabilities at the same time. You need to instil in your customer's organization a belief in a common future, one in which your superior capabilities and agility will make a difference in your customer's success. You need to make your customers dream, because you are a selling them a common future,

Figure 11.2 To support their transformation journeys, buyers search for innovation partners with high-end capabilities. They need a supplier classification that emphasizes future capabilities. This changes the role and the importance of personal power

something that doesn't tangibly exist yet. That requires a well-trained level of personal power.

At the same time, you face the risk that at least some, if not all, of your current sales volume might be reallocated to the lower right quadrant. This happens if, in the eyes of your buyer, your portfolio is good for today, but less relevant for their future. Once again, the time a buyer spends with a particular supplier will serve as a valuable indicator for that assessment. You should therefore watch out for changes in buyer's behaviour and be aware of when they start devoting less attention and time to you.

The balance of personal power versus paper power

The more the nature of your relationship progresses toward the top half of Figure 11.2, the more important your personal power becomes. In the top-left quadrant, a supplier may be small, but plays an important role in the buyer's value creation. The place where personal power plays its most important role – significantly outweighing the importance of paper power – is the top-right quadrant. Those suppliers may make a strong contribution to the customer's future through differentiation, ancillary services, and integration within the buyer's value chain, including product co-development. They may also have capabilities the buyer desires to access as part of their innovation or transformation agenda. This is a fundamentally different buyer–seller relationship than in any other quadrant.

In the lower-right quadrant, paper power tends to trump personal power, and you have little or no prospect of tipping the balance. Investing significantly in any form of personal power or building up personal capital is a waste of resources for either party. The best-case effect of personal power will be weak. Switching costs and a supplier's strategic importance tend to be low and objectively measurable, even when volumes are high. Price becomes the most important decision criterion, and there is little room to influence that number through personal power. Your best options are to change the frame by changing the choice architecture or taking advantage of other means to influence decisions, as we will describe in Part III.

Relationships in the lower-right quadrant can quickly develop a transactional character. When that happens, any give-and-take in the relationship must happen within the given transaction. There is no carryover to future transactions. Thus, the chances that personal power will make a difference are minimal or non-existent. In such cases, salespeople should focus on driving a direct *quid pro quo* and avoid any unsolicited investments (such as discounts or gifts) predicated on the hope that the buyer will remember it and reward it later.

How do you understand your position in the buyer's segmentation?

You need to recreate the buyer's segmentation on your own, as honestly and objectively as possible. This question goes beyond 'What role do you play for this customer?' or 'What value do you add?' and defines how they classify you internally and what criteria they use to make that classification. This means answering the following questions for every one of your customers.

- How many other options does the buyer have besides you?
- What capabilities do you have that the supplier finds attractive today and tomorrow?
- How important and valuable are you to the customer, both objectively and emotionally?
- What is the source of your real, enduring value?
- Are you hard to work with or easy to work with, in terms of ordering, service, replenishment, complaints, and so forth?

This line of thinking will help you determine whether you are a member of the vital few, the trivial many, or on the cusp between the two. Try to walk a mile in your customer's shoes, as the saying goes. Sometimes givens are not truly givens. The customer might value certain aspects that you or your salespeople might be taking for granted, and conversely, may attach little value to aspects you think are extremely important. Look back into the history between both companies for significant positive events.

If you find out that you have high relevance today but will probably have much less tomorrow, that will obviously be a bitter pill to swallow. All things considered, it is better to plan for obsolescence and focus on other customers than to wake up to obsolescence unprepared.

Let's now assume you have completed these assessments and have determined where your personal power has the strongest leverage. You haven't started to play offence until you have a plan to capitalize on that leverage. The next step in preparing that plan is understanding how buyers make their decisions, which leads us to Chapter 12.

Chapter 12

What Buyers Think and How They Make Decisions

There is a difference between a choice and a decision. A choice is the option that remains after someone applies a quintessential System 2 process: using a set of objective criteria systematically to eliminate alternatives. In contrast, a decision requires a judgment call, either because the application of objective criteria does not yield a clear result or because those criteria are too numerous or too tedious to review and weigh individually. Decisions invariably involve System 1 or ideally a blend of System 1 and System 2.

In today's world, objective product and service differentiation is harder than ever to achieve and maintain. Clear-cut choices tend to be the exception. Most commercial choices have way too many aspects for a normal human being to take into account. This makes it essential for salespeople to understand how and why buyers make decisions. Gaining that understanding represents a different kind of challenge for salespeople who are normally trained to lead a buyer to the best choice rather than to influence the buyer's decision.

Professional purchasing people, however, will not be easy targets for emotional appeals. Many of them will have well-honed procedures and processes designed to serve as lines of defence against subjective arguments that could influence their decisions. These defences make the salesperson's challenge more intricate, but certainly not insurmountable. The buyers' learned defences do not make them immune. They are human beings that share the same fundamental hard-wiring as everyone else. The better you understand and embrace the visible decision-making processes of the purchasing department, the more likely you are to discern its invisible inner workings as well. That will enable you to tailor your story to influence the frames that guide their decisions. Depending on your segment (see Figure 11.2), your basic intelligence gathering should start with these questions:

- **What does their rule book say?** Whether implicit or codified, every procurement organization has a defined way that it wants buyers to behave in front of suppliers. Their behaviour often offers clues to their systematic training. Are they aggressive on all fronts? Or do they push hard on some issues, while being softer in their personal interactions with you?
- **What is their true financial pain point?** When a buyer resists, it is easy to attribute their reaction to the price you are offering. But in some cases, the true pain point could be how cash-constrained they are, for example, and not how high your prices are. In such situations, you may be able to use terms and conditions or even time as a tactic to close the deal.
- **What is their organizational focus?** The organizational focus is where your customer applies the greatest scrutiny, the greatest pressure, and the strictest rules. It is also where they tend to express their greatest risk aversion. Look for opportunities to sell an advantage where there is currently less organizational focus. Think back to the 'monkey business' illusion we mentioned back in Situation 3.4. When a business is focused on one

area – its budget calendar, an implementation deadline, a quarterly quota – their focus narrows and they may ignore other aspects of the business.

What are buyers really thinking?

As we have said before, buyers are subject to the same behavioural, psychological, and neurobiological forces as sellers. This holds true whether you are Zooming with a negotiating partner you have known as a friend for years, or whether you are on a Microsoft Teams meeting in the chilling presence of an intimidating buyer.

In short, buyers are human too. In Part II, we highlighted the four universal phenomena that conspire to reinforce 'yes' as the salesperson's dominant response. In this section, we will highlight the four universal phenomena that make buyers more susceptible and thus more likely to buy your story and your offering:

1. It's harder to part with something than to acquire it.
2. It's hard to stop throwing good money after bad.
3. Price thresholds are personal, subjective, and often higher than you think.
4. People have a personal 'radar' that has room under it.

The simplicity of these statements belies just how deeply rooted and universal these effects are in human thinking.

1. It's harder to part with something than to acquire it

The term 'switching costs' sounds like a dry calculation better left to the financial or accounting teams. But switching costs have a powerful psychological side, as the Situation 12.1 demonstrates.

Situation 12.1: Maybe they can't live without us?

Halpero, Inc. is a market-leading manufacturer of construction materials.[1] It competes aggressively for every piece of business and has a reputation for squeezing its suppliers on price.

One morning Halpero's senior marketing executive, Sandra, welcomes a team of external consultants to a tour of the main production plants and warehouses. Once inside the main sorting and shipping facility, she waves her arm in an almost 180-degree arc to call attention to the mix of lift trucks and robots navigating the long corridors between the shelves.

'None of what you are looking at would work without our logistics supplier', she said. 'They know what we want better than we do ourselves, and every year they make us more efficient than even our best targets.'

The guests nod in agreement. While the logistics supplier isn't a household name, everyone in the party knows that it has a strong reputation for quality.

'Let's put it this way', Sandra concludes. 'If you work for them, please don't ever tell them that we would need to shut this place down tomorrow if they stopped serving us. We wouldn't exactly be dead, but losing them would set us back for a long time.'

We doubt that Sandra's colleagues in the procurement department would have made those kinds of remarks to anyone outside the company, but that doesn't mean they wouldn't agree with the remarks. The buyers at Halpero know that the value that the logistics supplier creates is tantamount to a trade secret. They have a strong interest in preventing that supplier's salespeople from appreciating just how well their company performs and how much leverage they truly have. This helps the buyers win in a negotiation by extracting lower prices and more concessions in the form of terms, conditions, product quality, and services.

The perceived value of the supplier relationship far exceeds the price Halpero pays for it. At the same time, Halpero's buyers are careful not to overplay their hand and risk undermining their advantage by pushing the supplier too far. They are reluctant to let go and to endure an uncomfortable breakup. They perceive the switching costs to be so prohibitively high that they do not even bother to calculate them.

What is the science behind this? The psychological force behind this perceived estimation of switching costs is the endowment effect. Thaler coined the term in 1980 to describe the situation when people demand much more to give up an object than they would be willing to pay to acquire it.[2] The endowment effect underscores how difficult it is for a newcomer to dislodge a valued incumbent supplier. It is also related to what Daniel Kahneman and Amos Tversky described as loss aversion: the negative utility of giving up an object is greater that the utility associated with acquiring it.[3] In 2001, Thaler and colleagues described the endowment effect as 'one of the most robust findings in the psychology of decision making'.[4]

What is our recommendation? Take the endowment effect into account as you assess your leverage in a negotiation. As Gaby described in the Introduction, she and her team understood this effect when they competed against Mr Anderson for Aurelio's business. There are objective 'paper' switching costs – such as testing, retooling, wind-down of existing supplies – that one can readily quantify in terms of time and money, but these calculations do not account for the mental switching costs, which play a noticeable role in whether a customer is willing to give up an existing relationship. This is especially relevant for small, high-end service businesses such as consultancies, agencies, lawyers, and accountants. These relationships are highly personal. It will take time for the customer to fill that void after a switch, even if the new partner offers an objectively measurable quality improvement. The intensity of these feelings is even higher when the incumbent is a company that has a history in solving acute problems for the customer. This is true in large companies as well as small ones.

The endowment effect therefore has several consequences for a sales negotiation, depending on whether the seller is the incumbent or the challenger. First, incumbent salespeople need to have up-to-date and honest answers to these segmentation questions we posed in Chapter 11. Only then can they determine the extent to which they can use their standing to their advantage in their negotiations. Second, the endowment effect can work in the incumbent's favour if they succeed in establishing and perpetuating a legacy in the customer organization, rather than merely a history.

The difference between legacy and history is that a legacy is a living history, as the next example shows. A large company developed and launched a new product in collaboration with a trusted supplier, but the product ran into severe technical difficulties that escalated to such an extent that observers started using the word 'scandal'. The original supplier was unable to solve the underlying problem, so the customer turned to a competing firm that ramped up quickly and solved the problem, albeit at a slightly higher price.[5] When the next round of negotiations with that 'heroic' supplier took place, the endowment effect ran deep. The customer was reluctant to give up on that supplier, even though it cost more to work with them.

The onus is now on the supplier to make sure that the endowment effect remains healthy. It is in the supplier's interest to turn that history into a legacy by incorporating it into its selling story and ensuring that the memory doesn't fade.

In general, you should keep the memory of joint victories and co-developed solutions alive in your regular interactions with clients and also make sure that these stories are used to help onboard new personnel. Make them campfire stories to be told from time to time so that everyone in the community – on both sides – can relate to the proud common past.

We cannot give incumbents a hard-and-fast rule on what the endowment effect and legacies mean in terms of prices. But you should think twice about reflexively granting a discount to an existing client – especially one with a strong legacy – simply because they ask. Loyalty discounts, for example, are not obligatory, although they can serve as good rewards when offered as small, unexpected gifts, as we will discuss in Chapter 15.

You may even want to play offence and look for ways to move your prices incrementally higher. In terms of making price increases or price adjustments, you could think of incorporating a slight 'friendship premium' and support it by showing how smoothly the business is running and your commitment to keeping it that way. Just don't use the phrase 'friendship premium' within earshot of your customers.

If you are the challenger, the odds are good that you will need to provide the customer a perceived benefit that is *subjectively* large enough to overcome the endowment effect and make them comfortable moving away from their existing supplier. This can mean providing credible assurances instead of money. This is where a strong brand can play a role. This essential reassurance strategy can include extra inventory, extra quality control, or having your service people on-premise during the initial changeover. You could also offer to monitor their customers' acceptance of a new formulation or new product that is using your materials or services. You can also show how your offering can help the customer acquire more customers for themselves. In any case, a lower price should be the last resort to overcome the endowment effect.

2. It's hard to stop throwing good money after bad

Imagine that you paid $800 six months ago to go on a trip next week. You planned to go with two friends, but you and your friends have drifted apart since you made the payment. To make matters worse, you are not feeling well at the moment, and you face some tight deadlines at work.

Would you still go on the trip?

The interesting finding is not how many people say they would still go. What is far more interesting is that significantly fewer people would go if they had won the trip in a raffle instead of paying $800.

This is one illustration of the sunk-cost fallacy. In a seminal paper on the topic, Ohio University researchers Hal Arkes and Catherine Blumer described the sunk-cost fallacy as, 'a greater tendency to continue an endeavor once an investment in money, effort, or time has been made'.[6] They also found that people 'who had incurred a sunk cost inflated their estimate of how likely a project was to succeed compared to the estimates of the same project by those who had not incurred a sunk cost'.[7]

In a business context, the sunk-cost fallacy means that people have a tendency to throw good money after bad, even if they have classic 'System 2' training or education that warns them they should know better. One challenge posed by Arkes and Blumer in their research demonstrates how pronounced this tendency is. They asked respondents to assume that they had just invested $10 million in a plane that radar cannot detect. As that project was 90% complete, the company learned that a competitor had started to market a new plane that is not only invisible to radar, but also much faster and more economical than the plane the respondents are developing. Nonetheless, some 82% of respondents said they would still invest to complete the original project, despite the recent news about its disadvantages.[8]

People run into difficulty with the sunk-cost fallacy, because System 1 longs for completion once we have made an investment into an idea or a project. The greater the prior investment is, the greater difficulties we will have to let go or move on if the future success of the project starts to look doubtful. One motivation for succumbing to the sunk-cost fallacy and continuing to invest is a reluctance to appear wasteful or to have one's name attached to failure. Another related factor is known as the planning fallacy, something nearly everyone experiences at some point. People tend to be exuberantly optimistic about how quickly they can complete a particular project, even when fully aware that they have often failed to complete similar projects on time in the past.

For some companies, the hardest question to answer is not 'What should we do?' but rather 'What should we stop doing?' Research into the sunk-cost fallacy and the planning fallacy show that the presence of a devil's advocate can help someone overcome their biases and stop throwing good money after bad.

Salespeople can start the devil's advocate process by viewing the market through the eyes of their customers' customers. Where is that market heading? Incumbents can offer alternatives to help the customer redirect resources in order to improve success chances of other existing projects or invest in different solutions. Depending on the stakes, approaching a customer can require either extreme boldness or extreme honesty. It can also involve finding other trusted allies within the buyer's organization and staging a friendly intervention to convince them to shift resources away from the quicksand of sunk-cost projects.

The sunk-cost fallacy has several consequences for a salesperson. The first is the fact that buyers – as representatives of their companies – will inevitably ask for some wasteful and unwise investments in projects. There is a reason why these investments are often called 'pet projects'. Their appeal is emotional and the desire for them to succeed is hard-wired into us.

Salespeople also need to be wary of the risk of the sunk-cost fallacy in their own work. It is not uncommon for salespeople to justify a lower price or discount by citing a buyer's promise of some future commitment: higher volumes, better terms, inside tracks to new projects, and so on. One could thus view a discount as an investment in a buyer's promise. Without outside guidance or a devil's advocate, a salesperson can find it challenging to abandon such decisions, even though most have little or no chance of working in the salesperson's favour. In some cases, it can even make sense to let a customer go. Salespeople need to recognize this and have the courage to know when to stop investing in false promises.

Let's take a timeout

Before we continue with the third and fourth points, pause for a moment and ask yourself what you should *stop* doing. You can think about this personally or professionally. In either case, we would be surprised if you didn't identify at least one project, initiative, or investment that qualifies as a textbook example of the sunk-cost fallacy or the planning fallacy.

3. Price thresholds are personal, subjective, and often higher than you think

In a sales environment, salespeople and buyers may describe prices and price thresholds in terms of pain. Whether it is bluff or not, a buyer might greet a price quote with a wince or a shudder or say 'that will hurt' when confronted with a price they perceive as too high or when they want to create the impression that the price is too high.

Are these thresholds real? Is the sensation of pain real? The answer lies within our brains. Studies of the price-quality heuristic, which we introduced at the beginning of Part II, have revealed that prices can cause perceptible pleasant sensations in our brains. The work that Kai did in the Starbucks study and subsequent experiments showed the existence of a feel-good price in our brains, which is technically a threshold. The price that elicits the strongest feeling in our minds might be significantly higher than the price we would consciously admit to in an open question or in another form of research.

Our answer is that real thresholds exist, but they rarely lie where our System 2 mind thinks they do. Sometimes we let the ghost of *homo economicus* whisper in our ears and tell us where various mathematical thresholds exist, such as maximum willingness to pay, the highest price that 'the market will bear', the profit-optimal selling price, or the floor price for a given negotiation. This is useful information, but it is only one set of guidance. The following story – adapted from a study that the neuroscience research agency Neurensics conducted – illustrates the deeper power that perceived thresholds exert.[9]

An insurance company relied on the broker model to sell policies and financial products despite the growth of direct-to-customer business models. Product management struggled in an internal discussion with upper management about whether the insurance should be priced above €99 per year for certain risk profiles. The stakeholders were split on whether a threshold existed at €100.[10]

Classic marketing research could not resolve the matter. In traditional pricing research, study participants are either explicitly asked to name a price, evaluate a given price, or select a product in a price choice architecture designed by the researcher. In all cases, the participants are aware of the goals of the study. Hence, all standard pricing research methods suffer from significant biases.[11]

Now think back to the wine and coffee experiments with brain wave testing at the start of Part II. The insurance company asked Neurensics to apply the same approach in order to understand the perceived value of their customers. Neurensics tested 40 typical customers and found – to their initial surprise – that there was no threshold in the minds of the customers. In the corresponding demand model, a substantial proportion of customers buy at prices of €105 or even up to €110 and beyond.

The insurance company then adjusted its software to present the brokers out in the field with some prices below €99 and some prices above. Analysing this dataset, it turned out that – as another unexpected surprise – the insurance sales dropped drastically at prices in the three-digit range. That means, out in the field there clearly was a threshold when increasing the price from €99 to €100.

What could explain this apparent contradiction? The insurance company wanted to know, so it commissioned another study, this time using the brokers on-site as study participants, not the customers. The brokers' brain responses were measured and their match-mismatch signals with respect to the pricing of the insurance were assessed. The results are depicted in Figure 12.1.

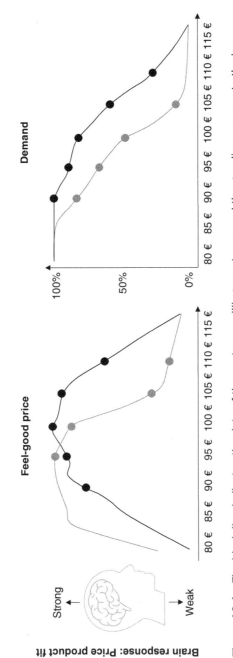

Figure 12.1 The black line indicates the data of the customer willingness-to-pay and the grey line represents the brokers. The feel-good-price curve shows a significant drop in broker's price perception at €100. The demand model shows a drastic decline at that level, indicating a typical pricing threshold

The brain signals revealed the threshold at €100 in the brokers' minds, corresponding remarkably well to the observation of the actual market data. The broker's value perception was lower than the typical customer's value perception of the financial product. This was a self-inflicted stress factor. Price discomfort is often at its peak when a price approaches a threshold and emotions create artificial barriers. People shy away from the risk of getting too close to a real or imagined threshold. In this case, the brokers feared the consequences of crossing a threshold more than their customers did. These findings imply that many organizations fall short of achieving the feel-good price because their salespeople are standing in their own way.

Using a combination of in-person coaching and media material, the insurance company coached the brokers to trust in the high value perception of the end customer, which was substantially reinforced by the brain data. This led to significantly improved sales numbers.

4. There really is room under someone's personal 'radar'

How much is $15 worth to you?

The ghost of *homo economicus* would whisper in your ear that '$15 is worth $15', perhaps followed with a 'duh!' for emphasis. It seems hard to argue with that logic, but Kahneman and Tversky nonetheless gave it a try in a thought experiment, which we have adapted for presentation here.

Let's say that you want to buy a package of pens for $30, but on the way to the store, you notice that another retailer is selling the same pack of branded pens for $15. Most customers would turn around and walk or drive a reasonable distance to buy the less expensive pens at the other store. Now let's say that you are going to buy a suit or a dress for $500 and then you realize that a nearby shop sells the outfit for $485. In that case, you are much less likely to walk or drive the same reasonable distance to the other store to buy the product there.

Why are some people willing to invest some effort to save $15 in one situation, but refuse to expend the same exact effort to save $15 in a different situation? For the explanation, we turn not to Kahneman and Tversky, but to a pair of nineteenth-century German scientists named Ernst Weber and Gustav Fechner. They discovered that in order for someone to perceive a difference between two stimuli, there needs to be a minimum difference between them.[12] If you lift two items, there has to be a minimum variation of 2% between the weights for you to perceive them as different. Weber also formulated a law that says that this ratio remains constant within reasonable ranges. In other words, the larger the weight, the larger the absolute difference needs to be for someone to notice. In the case of the $15 difference above, a 50% discount on a box of pens is clearly noticeable, but a 3% difference on the price of an outfit does not exert enough pull to entice someone to buy.[13]

These percentages differ by sense. The minimum difference for saltiness is as high as 8%, meaning you need 8% more salt to taste a difference between two soups or sausages. If there is less variation, the saltier product lies below what is known as the 'just noticeable difference'. The additional level of salt goes unnoticed.[14]

In terms of prices, one could refer to these differences as the 'just actionable difference' instead of 'just noticeable difference'. It implies that buyers have a certain radar that defines their sensitivity to price changes, whether up or down. If the magnitude of a price increase remains below the buyer's radar, the chances are higher that you can implement the change with less effort. The same thinking applies to discounts. A discount that is small may be the equivalent of the proverbial tree falling in the forest. If no one notices, did the falling tree (or falling price) really make a sound?

If you find yourself in a situation when a discount or lower price could make strategic or tactical sense, you need to make sure that the amount is sufficiently high to have the intended effect, or even have any effect at all. Ask yourself: Will this move really turn the situation to my favour? How will that happen? Offering a small discount that is 'below the radar' is tantamount to discreetly slipping money into their buyers' pockets when they aren't looking.

Chapter 13

What Is Your Re-pricing Strategy?

U nless you work for a company that is constantly launching new products, nearly all the products and services you sell already have a price attached to them. That means that your job requires you to re-price something rather than to set a price for it. When you are on offence, your re-pricing actions will fall into one of two categories, depending on your underlying cost basis:

- **Price increases:** You attempt to raise prices without a change in your costs. A successful price increase will boost your gross margin.
- **Price adjustments:** You attempt to raise prices in response to a change in your costs (usually an increase). These are common moves during a period of persistent inflation. The primary motivation behind price adjustments is to protect margins rather than increase them.

This distinction is important, because many behavioural, psychological, and neuroscientific forces come into play when buyers encounter a price change. Perception and reality can easily clash if they misunderstand or misinterpret your actions. That's why you need a re-pricing strategy to help you take advantage of the power of price increases and price adjustments.

The power of price increases

As most salespeople understand, if you approach a customer with a blunt in-your-face attempt to increase prices, buyers will most likely perceive it as an obvious and perhaps even brazen attempt to gain more margin. If they feel a potential sense of loss or think that the supplier is trying to take advantage of them, they will be more suspicious and less forgiving.

A price increase is less obtrusive when the revenue pie in the market is growing quickly and the seller wants to gain a greater or 'fairer' share of that growing pie. In markets with little or no growth, however, a price increase raises legitimate questions: does the higher price reflect a supply-and-demand imbalance, such as a current or looming scarcity? Is the seller's viability or survival at risk for some undisclosed reason? Or is the seller simply seeking to improve its bottom line?

Price increases do indeed have a significant effect on profit. To illustrate this inherent power of price increases, we turn on System 2 and derive a break-even table similar to the ones we showed for discounts in Chapter 7. Table 13.1 shows what happens to profit when you increase prices by a certain amount, then sell enough units to keep revenue constant. Remember that because this is a price increase, we assume that unit costs remain constant.

Let's assume you are attempting to raise prices by 5%. To achieve the same amount of revenue as before, you can afford to sell 5% fewer units, but even with that slight loss of volume, your profit would increase by 19%. The higher margin per unit more than offsets the lower volume. The higher the price increase, the more dramatic the profit improvement becomes. With a price increase of 15%, you could lose as much as 13% of your

Table 13.1 What happens to profit when prices rise, but unit cost and revenue remain constant? (All figures except volume change rounded to the nearest full amount; revenue rounded to $10,000 for simplicity's sake)

Price Increase	Revenue in US$	Price in US$	Volume		Unit Cost in US$	Profit in US$	
			Units	Change		Amount	Change
0%	10,000	100	100	0.0%	80	2,000	0%
3%	10,000	103	97	−3.0%	80	2,231	12%
5%	**10,000**	**105**	**95**	**−5.0%**	**80**	**2,375**	**19%**
10%	10,000	110	91	−9.0%	80	2,730	37%
15%	10,000	115	87	−13.0%	80	3,045	52%
18%	10,000	118	85	−15.0%	80	3,230	62%
20%	10,000	120	83	−17.0%	80	3,320	66%
25%	10,000	125	80	−20.0%	80	3,600	80%

volume and still hit the same revenue target. Your profit, however, would increase by 52%. The System 2 perspective can make price increases very tempting if you are willing to sacrifice the amount of volume shown in Table 13.1.

Some companies may have an opportunity for price increases when macroeconomic and market trends create a seller's market. How buyers interpret the macroeconomic and market situation naturally influences their feel-good price and thus your ability to get closer to a desired price level. Seller's markets often occur as a result of an imbalance between supply and demand, such as shortages in raw materials, delays in shipping, or a lack of available talent. Sellers can use this as a chance to implement a price increase.

The balance of personal and paper power can help you access your risk of volume loss on a case-by-case basis. This can ease your fears of retaliation in terms of losing current or future business. Situation 12.1 and the Neurensics example in Chapter 12 show that sellers can underestimate how much power they have to raise prices if they don't fully understand their importance to the customer or if they imagine thresholds where none exist. This is why the analyses we described in Chapter 11 should become a habit. Prior to a price increase attempt, you should analyse your business relationship with a particular customer to evaluate the true risk.

The power of price adjustments

After many years when companies and markets flourished thanks to stability in main macroeconomic drivers, the 2020s ushered in a period characterized by much less economic stability. Until there is a return to longer periods of stability, sellers will have to embrace the challenge of making more frequent price changes to minimize the risks to their business. Such periods usually warrant price adjustments instead of price increase.

Price adjustments convey a more neutral tone and reflect the seller's adaptation to cost changes rather than an attempt to achieve higher margins. Table 13.2 shows one example for a price adjustment. Let's assume that your variable unit costs increase by the amounts shown, and in each case, you adjust prices upward by the same amount in percentage terms. For example, if unit costs rise by $10 from $80 to $90, that is a percentage increase of 13%. If you adjusted your prices by 13% to compensate, you can afford a volume loss of up to 11% with that price adjustment and still keep revenue and profit constant.

The role of fairness

The old cliché in business is that the customer is king, but behavioural economics, psychology, and neuroscience tell us that the customer is human. That can make all the difference in how they perceive your attempts to change prices.

Table 13.2 Volume required to keep revenue, gross margin percentage, and profit constant after passing on a cost increase to customers in full through a corresponding price adjustment. (All figures rounded to the nearest full amount; revenue rounded to $10,000 and profit to $2,000 for simplicity's sake)

Price Adjustment	Revenue in US$	Price in US$	Volume		Unit Cost in US$		Gross margin	Profit in US$
			Units	Change	Amount	Change		
0%	10,000	100	100		80		20%	2,000
4%	10,000	104	96	−4	83	4%	20%	2,000
6%	10,000	106	94	−6	85	6%	20%	2,000
13%	**10,000**	**113**	**89**	**−11**	**90**	**13%**	**20%**	**2,000**
19%	10,000	119	84	−16	95	19%	20%	2,000
25%	10,000	125	80	−20	100	25%	20%	2,000
31%	10,000	131	76	−24	105	31%	20%	2,000
38%	10,000	138	72	−27	110	38%	20%	2,000

Vikas Mittal and his colleagues at Rice University surveyed more than 7,900 B2B customers and report that getting a fair price is three times more important to respondents than getting the lowest price.[1] Meanwhile, a survey of over 13,000 people in eight countries conducted by BCG's Bruce Henderson Institute concluded that the reaction of consumers to prices is 'usually asymmetric. Making a fair price slightly fairer may bring little incremental benefit, while even slight missteps in terms of unfairness can draw a strong negative reaction from consumers'.[2]

This begs the question of how to define a fair price. Mittal and his colleagues describe a fair price as 'you are not priced at the extreme (highest or lowest), the pricing structure is easy to understand and the price is closer to industry-sector average (slightly higher is OK)'.[3] BCG says that '[w]hether individuals perceive a price to be fair will depend on the product or service category, their age, where they live, what they earn, their political beliefs, and who the customer is (themselves or someone else).'

These somewhat ambiguous definitions, in turn, beg another question: is there an innate and common human response to fairness? Several studies seem to indicate the answer is 'yes'.[4]

One study run at Matthew Lieberman's lab in Los Angeles used a variation of the Ultimatum Game to understand monetary fairness. In the Ultimatum Game, one participant – called the proposer – has a chance to receive a certain amount of money, which they can split any way they want with another participant, called the responder. The responder can either accept the proposed deal or reject it, with no negotiation permitted.

Let's say the researcher says that Andrea can receive $10. Andrea decides to keep $6 and offer the remaining $4 to Mandy. If Mandy accepts, each receives their money. If Mandy rejects the proposal, neither Andrea nor Mandy receives any money.

Lieberman and his colleagues tested the emotional reaction of responders in psychological experiments and in the MRI scanner. Both the psychological assessment as well as the fMRI brain scans indicated that responders were particularly happy when they perceived the split to be particularly fair, say 50:50. The absolute monetary gain, however, had much less impact on the reward networks of the brain.

This study has two implications for a salesperson playing the Invisible Game. First, fairness is very important for a creating and maintaining a positive relationship. Second, fairness is a mental construct associated much more tightly with how someone feels than with the absolute amounts of money involved, regardless of how high.[5]

Buyers are trained to resist price increases, but as we have conveyed throughout the book so far, prices are much more than numbers. They form only one aspect of the buyer's decision-making process. Buyers generally view price adjustments, however, as fairer than price increases when they have a valid justification or story behind them. That story can build on the fact that rising costs can put a supplier at a disadvantage that requires some form of fair correction or shared burden. Such an 'in-need' argument for a price adjustment should signal to the buyer at a pre-conscious level that the request for a price adjustment is fair.

The challenge lies in bringing perception in sync with reality. When you present your price adjustment as unavoidable due to cost changes, the painful plea of 'we need extra help' should look and feel like pain in every way. Adapt your body and written language accordingly, and don't show up to a meeting behind the wheel of a brand-new luxury company car. In every case, the congruence between the story and price must remain intact. Semantics matter. System 2 as always tells one side of the story. It helps set the guardrails and defines how a realized price translates into other financial terms such as revenue and profit. But the right story triggers the right System 1 response and appeals to a buyer's sense of fairness.

Your story should also take the customer's organizational focus into account, as we discussed in the previous chapter. Your customer's biggest pain may not even be price but cash. One of our clients told us a few years ago about a customer whose only concern was the implementation date of the price adjustment, not its amount. They were so concerned about getting to the end of their fiscal year without a price change that they accepted the proposed amount without a challenge. The price change was then implemented during the next fiscal year. Such a response reflects what we refer to as 'the power of now' and a concept called hyperbolic discounting, which we will look at in more detail in Chapter 16.

Time can work to your advantage when you implement price changes. Success comes from managing both the clock and the calendar. You don't artificially increase the stress on the buyer, but rather make your offers or requests at a time when buyers will be most receptive to a change. The best time to ask for money is when money is in flux, which is usually during budget planning season. Because companies have constrained budgets, asking for changes off-cycle could have little chance of doing anything except damaging the relationship. One way to make these discussions a habit and reduce their anxiety is to establish a pricing calendar for the entire year. This makes price discussions a natural habit for you and for the buyer as well.

Large companies have entire departments to worry about re-pricing, but small-business owners or trusted consultants must do the job themselves and often overlook or are too shy to raise their prices regularly. They can also use the clock and the calendar to their advantage. Small-business owners and service providers should benchmark their service – including the segmentations we described in Chapter 11 – two or three months before the end of their fiscal year. This gives you time to communicate what your prices or fees will be for the coming year.

Raising prices without raising prices

Regardless of whether you are striving for a price increase or a price adjustment, you can't succeed unless you change the frame, change the story, or use other means to influence their buying decision in your favour. In the remainder of Part III, we will provide advanced techniques that you can use to exert that influence. In some cases, you can increase your revenue and profit without raising prices at all.

Chapters 14 and 15 will elaborate on more of the fundamental behavioural, psychological, and neuroscientific insights that help you play offence and influence buyers. Chapters 16 to 18 will introduce techniques that reframe what behavioural economists refer to as a choice architecture. In a paper simply called 'Choice architecture', Thaler and his colleagues wrote: 'Decision makers do not make choices in a vacuum. They make them in an environment where many features, noticed and unnoticed, can influence their decisions. The person who frames that environment is, in our terminology, a choice architect.'[6]

Every sales negotiation has a choice architect, and we recommend strongly that you play that role. Remember that the party that makes the first move usually establishes and maintains the frame for the negotiation. But establishing that frame is only an initial step. A home-field advantage is meaningless if you don't have a game plan and execute it well, and that means re-framing as well. The most effective choice architectures will allow buyers to feel good about paying the price you wanted them to pay all along.

You will recall from Part II that human beings – whether they are experienced professional buyers or teenage consumers browsing in a shopping portal – must learn how to perceive and assess the prices they observe. No one should interpret your prices without scales and stories that you have provided. You can help people with their learning processes by creating and controlling the options they see by using techniques such as anchoring, the Power of 3, the power of free, decoys, bundling, and unbundling. We will explore these and other concepts rigorously and show their practical application. Part III will the conclude with a chapter that describes some additional and often overlooked tactics that you can use to influence the course of a negotiation and its aftermath.

Well-trained buyers will use many tactics to assert their own strategies and avoid surrendering their positions. It is not only important for you to recognize these tactics and counter them, but also play offence by balancing gains, concessions, and uncertainty to your own advantage.

Chapter 14

Who Will You Anchor Today?

A salesperson's most important tool for influencing prices is anchoring, which we introduced at the end of Part I. The power of anchoring is the basis for our recommending 'Make the first move!', rather than waiting to see what price the customer uses to establish the reference price or anchor that will guide the rest of the negotiation.

However, you can't simply throw out any high price as an anchor just to make subsequent prices look more appealing. Setting an anchor presents several challenges. What specific customer behaviour do you want your anchor to encourage? Everything else derives from your answer to that question. You need to be clear on how you want the buyer to understand the anchor and how they will incorporate it into their decision making, so that you can avoid misinterpretations. You also need to maintain a consistent credible link between price and value, limit the buyer's ability to directly compare offerings, and avoid letting your anchors become less potent due to familiarity.

These guidelines will enable you to address these challenges and tap into the tremendous power of anchoring effectively and ethically.

- **Anchors are not target prices:** The anchor price serves as a reference point, not a selling point. Customer familiarity and the nature of the relationship will define the separation between these two price points. The less familiar the buyer is with an offering, the stronger the influence of your reference price will be and the more latitude you will have to set it. If the buyer is more familiar with the offering, the anchor should reflect a fully valued price. The fully valued price means that the seller retains all the value instead of sharing some of the offering's added value with the buyer. The ultimate selling price is a way to calibrate who gets what share. Finally, setting an anchor will also depend on whether the negotiation is transactional – meaning each side is trying to maximize its take within that single deal – or whether the relationship is ongoing, which means the anchor will carry over to future transactions.

- **Anchors need anchors:** The anchor in the fundraising experiment in Singapore (see Chapter 4) was linked to a plausible level of value. Such anchors help potential buyers determine whether a price–value relationship is fair and reasonable, and then decide whether they should act on it. This is especially important when prices are not transparent or customer uncertainty is high.

- **Make anchoring a habit:** Anchoring is more than an important technique. It should become a habit, something that you work at daily, both in terms of awareness and action. Awareness is important, because in the Invisible Game in order to create and control the frames of a negotiation, all parties – you, your customers, and competitors – are trying to gain an edge. When any company makes a public statement about price levels, that form of anchoring is known as signalling. Many industries, especially highly concentrated ones with only slight differentiation across products, usually have at least one company that makes regular public announcements about the future course of prices, either by announcing specific changes or by citing major trends that would warrant price changes. Both your customers and your competitors give you signals that are cues for setting your own specific anchors for your next negotiation. If the public announcements are about trends rather than specific price points, suppliers have an opportunity to assess those trends and get ahead of the curve.

- **Anchors can wear out:** Few things are more frustrating for salesperson than trying to sell a next-generation product when the buyers are relying on past-generation price anchors. But that is happening with increasing frequency. In the 2020s, almost all markets have become more dynamic, with shorter product life cycles, lower barriers to entry, and greater access to information. In these situations, you don't want a price anchor to become analogous to a physical anchor, something that prevents your business from moving forward. Gone are the slow-moving 'good old days' when markets had a stable balance of power and an established set of competitors, customers, and products. The more dynamic your market is, the more strategically you need to manage your anchor prices and the more frequently you will need to review and change them.
- **You often need an integrated system of anchors:** Anchors not only help buyers distinguish between your prices and your competitors' but also across your own portfolio of products and services. That means that you cannot successfully set anchors without taking into account their effect on your entire portfolio.
- **Anchors also calibrate future negotiations, not just current ones:** The most successful pricing stories follow a long narrative arc – with future moves already plotted far ahead of time – rather than a collection of short stories and episodes involving the same characters. The ability to do that is part of the mastery of pricing.

Setting an anchor can become an ongoing process. Different contexts throughout the year – dinners, social events, industry conferences – create opportunities to make subtle references to anchors. Indirect references to leading indicators, commodity forecasts, gross domestic product (GDP), or other data help create a space for your stories and numbers to live in. This increases the chances that your anchor not only becomes *their* anchor, but also becomes the basis for calculating any just actionable differences.

One form of anchoring that reflects all of these challenges acutely is the list price. List prices were the dominant form of price communication in pre-internet days, when printed catalogues and price sheets provided buyers with their initial cues on prices. List prices can still serve as important anchors in markets with greater complexity or whenever prices are less comparable. This is especially true for service businesses. But list prices carry a greater risk in more commoditized businesses or in situations when professional procurement drives the decision. The issue is the ability to compare prices quickly. While this was always done in the days of printed catalogues, online research allows purchasers to compare multiple list prices instantaneously and immediately exclude companies that appear to be outliers. In other words, your list prices can eliminate you from competition before you ever have an opportunity to speak with the customer.

The key issue is the price–value relationship that your list price is supposed to express. Are you establishing the highest price for your largest premium? Are you providing customers with a standard price for a standard product, knowing that most of your customers will add or subtract some form of customization to make their product (and thus their ultimate price) unique?

The standards you set – and the value drivers that support them – won't be clear to buyers unless they are also clear to everyone in your company. Likewise, everyone in your company must be clear on when you can deviate from these standards. If you have the premium anchor, you will need a system for allowing prices and features to deviate from the maximum. If you have standard prices, the final price may be lower if the customer places a large single order or hits a volume threshold in a given period. Likewise, the customer may receive a lower price to encourage or reward behaviours that improve your operational efficiency, such as standard consistent orders versus less than truckload, or standard delivery versus faster or slower delivery. Conversely, they could face higher prices or sur-charges if their requests – especially for services – deviate significantly from standards. The common thread here is that any discount should involve reciprocity, or at least the appearance of reciprocity. As we dis-cussed in Chapter 11, the nature of your relationship with the buyers will determine whether that reciprocity occurs over time – across multiple transactions – or is confined to one transaction (tit-for-tat.)

Companies with large portfolios will need multiple anchor prices, and therefore multiple list prices if they decide to make their prices public and transparent. Anchor prices need to make sense individually and collectively in order to have the desired effects on customer behaviour.

Chapter 15

Why Equal Things Aren't Always Equal

Imagine you are confronted with the following proposition: you can either accept $1,800 with no strings attached, or you can opt for a 90% chance to win $2,000, which means you have a 10% chance of coming away empty handed. Which option would you prefer?

Now let's flip things around. This time, your two options are either to lose $1,800, or to have a 90% chance of losing $2,000, which means you have a 10% chance of suffering no loss at all. Which option would you prefer?

If you are like most people, your chosen option in both cases would reflect the natural human tendencies toward risk aversion. Humans are risk-averse when it comes to gains, but risk-seeking when it comes to losses. The usual response to the first question is to take the money and run, rather than risk that money for a somewhat larger gain. If you have spent time watching game shows, you have seen contestants wrestle with that question and have probably implored them to 'Take the money!' But in the second situation, people want to avoid the certain loss, and take their chances – however slight – that they might lose nothing at all. These sharp preferences hold true even though – purely mathematically speaking – there was no difference between any of the options above. Players either had an expected loss or an expected gain of $1,800.

This example derives from prospect theory, which we introduced briefly in Chapter 8, when we demonstrated with a practical example that losing hurts more than winning excites, even when the spoils are equal. What is even more fascinating about prospect theory is that risk aversion guides our thinking even when the stakes are unequal. In his seminal paper with Tversky, Kahneman cites a similar example: respondents need to choose between an 80% chance of losing $4,000 or a certain loss of $3,000. They write that 'the majority of subjects were willing to accept a risk of .80 to lose 4,000, in preference to a sure loss of 3,000, although the gamble has a lower expected value.'[1]

Do these experiments into basic human-decision science have any practical value for sales negotiations in the twenty-first century? Yes, they do!

Prospect theory – which summarizes the breadth of these findings so neatly – has three basic tenets:

- Small values in gains and losses have a disproportionately high psychological impact.
- High values in gains and losses have a disproportionately low psychological impact.
- People suffer from losses more than they enjoy gains.

According to prospect theory, people feel that the negative utility of a loss outweighs the positive utility of a gain of the same magnitude. If the stakes are equal, we emphasize loss avoidance over the pursuit of gain. This validates the age-old cliché that a bird in the hand is worth two in the bush. These insights culminate in a graph plotting 'real financial value' (expressed as dollar amounts) on the x axis and 'psychological value' on the y axis, as shown in Figure 15.1.

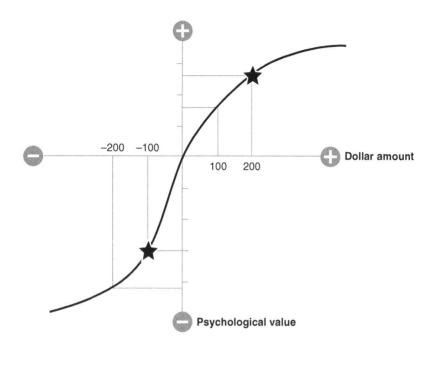

Figure 15.1 The famous prospect theory curve – developed by Kahneman and Tversky – illustrates the different values of gains and losses[2]

The first thing to note in Figure 15.1 is that the ghost of *homo economicus* would disagree with the shape of the curve. The ghost would consider anything but a straight line to be perplexing. After all, logic demands that $100 is $100. But this is not the case, because $100 doesn't always feel like $100.

The first $100 you pay hurt a lot, but at higher values, there is little psychological impact. For instance, most people would be extremely frustrated if they dropped a $100 dollar bill in a storm drain and could not recover it. Yet those very same people would worry to the same extent over a 5% fee for a real estate broker when buying a house. Humans perceive money as relative. Paying $315,000 instead of $300,000 for a house appears to be of a comparable psychological magnitude as losing that $100 bill in the storm drain.

Financial gains are also disproportionately valued, in the sense that small gains are valued relatively more than large gains. This is why the curve in Figure 15.1 is S-shaped. Furthermore, the S-shaped curve is *asymmetric*. For a better understanding we have added two stars to the original graph. Take the little star in the lower-left quadrant: losing $100 feels like losing $300. Check out the star in the upper-right quadrant: winning $200 feels like winning $280. That is more than the $200 face value, but still less than the perceived loss of $300. That is why most people would reject a random coin-flipping match with a 2:1 payoff with a random stranger on the street.

So how specifically can prospect theory help change the course of a sales negotiation? As you can imagine, insights into how people assess risks and perceive gains and losses have powerful practical applications. The theory offers clear guidance on some eternal questions that don't seem to have an answer that everyone can agree on: should we deliver bad news or good news first? Should we emphasize the language of hope, which means that we highlight the benefits of our offering? Or should we use the language of fear and highlight the customer's pain points? Should we dangle the promise of a big gain down the road or give our customer a smaller reward now? Situations 15.1 and 15.2 explore these questions.

Situation 15.1: Shall we split up a planned price increase in order to soften the blow?

We have been planning a price increase for quite some time, for several reasons. We have a sense that we are undervalued in the market, and we have noticed signals from our market and competitive intelligence that customers could absorb the higher prices. The final straw was input cost inflation, which put pressure on our margins.

We settled on an increase of 6% on our core products, but now our manager insists on breaking that up into smaller increments. Our last few meetings seem to be nothing but discussions around whether it should be 3-2-1 or 2-2-2, or even staged at 1% per month for half a year. His rationale is always that we don't want get our customers upset, and he uses the old 'boiling the frog' story: the customer may eventually realize they are cooked, but they won't notice it while they are cooking.[3] What should we do?

What is the science behind this? The idea that it is better to 'drizzle' bad news is misguided, because the negative impact of small costs is disproportionally high. This is a classic application of prospect theory. The chart in Figure 15.1 – adapted from Kahneman and Tversky's seminal paper 'Prospect theory: an analysis of decision under risk' – is stylized, but it illustrates the simple arithmetic behind bad news and good news.[4] Price increases are perceived losses and thus have a negative psychological impact on customers. Their impact is shown in the lower-left quadrant. The cumulative psychological impact of two $100 losses is much greater than the impact of one $200 loss.

What is our recommendation? Bring pain and perceived losses such as price increases to your client in one go, so that your client can process the pain quickly and move on. Having said that, you should also take steps to cushion the blow that you deliver all at once. To influence perception, make the magnitude of the price increase seem as small as possible, whether it is expressed as a percentage, and absolute amount, or a relative change. You can support these small numbers with analogies that make the numbers seem smaller or even trivial, such as expressing the prices in terms of subway rides, slices of pizza, or cups of coffee. You can also make pricing discussions part of your annual calendar, so the client gets used to the process of price changes. It is easier for customers to accept price increases when they sync it with their own budgeting calendars.

The asymmetric S-shaped curve of prospect theory comes with a further complication that is highly relevant for the sales relationship: the zero-point is adjustable. Different scenarios tested by Kahneman and Tversky showed that our expectations shift the zero point. Practically speaking, this means that unexpected gains have a greater impact than expected benefits. Surprising a loyal long-term client with small free shipment of goods can make them very happy and strengthen the relationship disproportionately.

Now let's take a look at a situation when someone has good news to deliver. How do you expect the approach to differ in this situation?

Situation 15.2: We have streamlined our cost structure. This is great news! How should we tell our customers about it?

Thanks to Six Sigma and re-engineering efforts, we have optimized our cost structure significantly. We can use this competitive advantage to reduce our prices for key accounts or to gain access to business areas that we were too expensive or too inefficient for us to compete in before. The challenge lies

In breaking this news to customers. We have so much to say that we could easily overwhelm them, but if we set our priorities right, we could launch a Big Bang announcement, pleasantly surprise our customers, and catch our competition flat-footed with no idea what to respond to.

What is the science behind this? This is the converse of what we described in the previous situation. Now let's home in on the upper-right quadrant of Figure 15.1. The law of diminishing returns sets in quickly when you announce good news or give customers a victory. In other words, the incremental impact of an additional aspect aggregated into a Big Win or Big Bang will always be less than if you presented that aspect separately. Prospect theory teaches us that small perceived gains are valued disproportionately highly.

What is our recommendation? Buyers share the same hard-wired reward system as every other human. That means that if you have a collection of benefits, rewards, or good news for your clients, the cumulative effect is greater if you drizzle them over time rather than deliver them all at once.

The previous two situations focused on how to deliver good news and bad news. The next two situations, in Chapter 16, show how prospect theory can affect how an organization sets its priorities, embraces new ideas, and plans for the future. Organizations, like people, have several strengths and weaknesses. Is it better for an organization to invest in enhancing a strength or overcoming a weakness? Perhaps even more important for planning and priorities: is it *easier* for an organization to enhance a strength or overcome a weakness?

Thanks to conventional training and the business media, suppliers and their salespeople are so laser-focused on adding value that they overlook opportunities to subtract pain. The phrase 'pain point' is a business buzzword, but it is also a strong behavioural driver. Given a choice between getting better at something good (enhancing a strength) or becoming 'less bad' at something you aren't as good at (overcoming a weakness), the latter can have the stronger psychological impact. You'll notice that the steepest part of the curve in Figure 15.1 – the place where the psychological impact is greatest relative to the change that caused it – is in the area of small losses. Sometimes addition by subtraction is an attractive approach.

Chapter 16

The Power of Free and the Power of Now

You and your customers are subject to a vast range of biases, more than we could ever hope to address in depth in our book. It would be both overwhelming and impractical for any book to help you tighten every mental bolt and screw so that you become aware of all your own biases, learn to resist them, learn to identify them in others, and then learn to apply that mastery and control to make your own negotiations more successful.

That forced us to decide which biases you should not only learn first, but also learn so well that you can try to make their use second nature. In this chapter we look at two important biases that directly and significantly affect how much money the parties will exchange in a negotiation. These biases are the zero-risk bias and the present bias. In layman's terms, they translate into power of free and the power of now.

Understanding and controlling these two biases will help you avoid the risks – the fears, game-playing, and price erosion – that conventional forms of discounting can lead to. Learning to say 'no' – one of the main accomplishments from Part II – does not mean that discounts have absolutely no role to play in a sales negotiation. When used in the right way and in the right context, they can help you defend prices, make customers happy, and encourage a longer-term relationship or partnership instead of a transactional one. In this sense, discounting is not a disease or sickness, but rather the science of giving money away for your own benefit.

The power of free

The cliché 'There's no such thing as a free lunch' condenses so much economic wisdom that Milton Friedman, the 1976 Nobel Prize winner, used it as the title for a book he published in the mid-1970s. It means that when someone receives a good or a service for free, someone ends up paying the bill or bearing the costs. That could even be the recipients themselves, who pay indirectly or pay later.

Does that mean that offering something for free is always a mistake? If so, it seems as if companies that we encounter every day as consumers are making a lot of mistakes! Amazon Prime is famous for its offer of 'free shipping'. Most retail stores have some variation of a 'buy one, get one free' offer. Even a small business such as a sandwich shop or a car wash will have a loyalty card that gives you something free when you have ordered, say, 8 sandwiches or 10 car washes.

System 2 tells us that free is nothing more than a price of zero. When *homo economicus* weighs benefits and costs, for example, free enters the calculus as a cost of zero. But Kristina Shampanier (MIT), Nina Mazar (University of Toronto), and Dan Ariely (Duke University) sensed that free exerts a stronger influence on decisions than people might suspect. In their study published in *Marketing Science*, they concluded that 'people appear to act as if zero pricing of a good not only decreases its cost, but also adds to its benefits.'[1] Free, in other words, has a positive intrinsic value all its own. Situation 16.1 provides an example.

Situation 16.1: 'To free or not to free'

When a catastrophic storm devastated a Caribbean island a few years ago, one of our customers chartered planes and shipped pallets of their core products to one of the hardest hit areas. Within 48 hours, they had helped thousands of victims meet some of their basic care needs.

This inspired us to make a gesture of goodwill to acknowledge their act of kindness. You think that should be easy to do!

But there is a huge debate raging in our company on how to package it. While I'm happy we are looking at other options besides writing them a nice cheque, I wish there was a way to impose some order on the discussion. We eventually boiled it down to three alternatives to a direct payment: we could offer them a discount, a rebate, or a shipment of free raw materials to replenish their supplies. Now the finance department insists that if we opt to send them 'free goods', the customer should still pay the freight costs. What is the best approach?

What is the science behind this? One way to interpret the study we just cited is that free is tantamount to a gift. The introduction of money into the context of a gift spoils the effect. Another paper co-authored by Ariely suggested that a price of zero (free) shifts the basis of an exchange from a market-based one to a social one.[2] To put this in a personal context, you might be willing to help a friend move to a different apartment, but the goodwill from that gift loses its lustre if you demand minimum wage for the work, or even if your friend offers to pay you a small amount.

What is our recommendation? The recommendation is to offer the free goods, but do not charge the customer for shipping. One side effect of offering free goods is that it protects the integrity of your prices. A discount or rebate directly linked to your product may affect the value perception of your offering to such an extent that customers may expect an outright price decrease later on. You effectively set a new anchor that works against you. Offering free goods also generates a level of goodwill, but only if the offer is really free. Asking for payment of freight charges flushes away the positive effect.

The power of now

The technical term for the power of now is hyperbolic discounting.[3] Situation 16.2 describes one of its most common applications.

Situation 16.2: Understanding the value of 'right now'

For a recent competitive bid, we developed a strong plan for common innovation and strong future growth. We were convinced that we had the best overall package, with a strong focus on the ongoing relationship. Then, to our surprise, a smaller competitor won the bid by delivering a number of small short-term benefits.

What is the science behind this? Human beings prefer fast rewards and late punishments. The emotional impact of something positive is higher the sooner it happens. The impact of something negative is worse the sooner it happens. Both effects, however, diminish over time. Our emotional response follows a hyperbolic curve, as shown in Figure 16.1. Think of it this way. If you offered someone a choice between $5 right now or $15 three months from now, their inclination would be to take the money rather than wait. But if you offered to give them $5 a year from now and $15 a year and three months from now, they would likely wait the extra three months and take the $15. Even though the time gap between the options is identical (three months), there is no feeling of 'now' anymore in the second situation.

What is our recommendation? Our evolutionary mindset cannot resist the short term. In any competitive bid, do not forget to weave in small, immediate, and tangible benefits into your proposal. Promises of future potential bigger gains have less impact on the reward network of our brain. Considering our brain's reaction to loss, it can be prudent to go for large price increases with delayed implementation dates. Such changes will be more palatable if you respect the client's budgeting calendar, which may be on a different timeline than yours. Do not always wait until the client is pushing through their demands for savings. Instead, look for opportunities to be courageous, and most importantly, proactive. A small immediate gratification offered to customers upfront may be a way to gain more – or get away with less – over time.

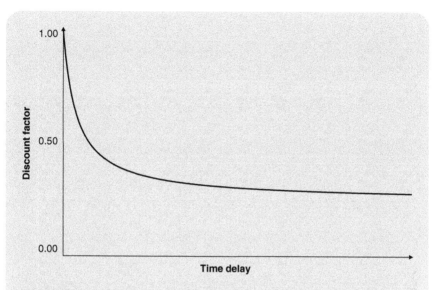

Figure 16.1 Hyperbolic discounting: this curve shows that people place higher value on near-term rewards, but lower value on the same reward at a later time

Opportunities to seize the power of now are widespread. The curve in Figure 16.1 allows you to make small positive amounts look larger – and have a greater perceived impact – and also make larger negative amounts look smaller by delivering them later. This can apply to bonuses and other rewards as well as to price increases and adjustments for currency fluctuations.

Chapter 17

To Bundle or Not to Bundle: Is That Really the Question?

The very question of whether a company should bundle or unbundle its products implies that at any given point in a product's life cycle, there is an ideal way to package the various products, product components, and services in a portfolio into appealing offers for customers.

The easiest association with bundling for most people is the combo meal they can order at a fast-food restaurant: a sandwich, a side dish, and a beverage, at a lower combined price than the items cost separately. This is an example of 'mixed bundling', which means that a customer can also purchase one or more of the components of the bundle individually. The classic physical music formats such as the compact disc and vinyl LP are also familiar bundles, but they exemplify 'pure bundling'. In contrast to mixed bundling, a pure bundle forces customers to buy the whole package – in this case, the whole album – even if they only want one or two songs. With some exceptions, the individual components are not available for sale separately.

So how should a company determine those ideal combinations of products and services in a portfolio and then sell them to customers? In the spirit of the Visible Game, companies can cite numerous practical and objective reasons to create bundles or break them up. These reasons include logistical and manufacturing efficiencies, easier and clearer communication, and the potential for better financial performance. Even so, there is also enormous untapped and overlooked potential for bundling and unbundling in the Invisible Game. In the rest of this chapter, we will highlight some of these influencing factors behind the art and science of bundling, before showing how companies can play the Invisible and Visible Games simultaneously to find – and adjust – their own balanced offerings with confidence. Some of the same principles apply to unbundling, and we will conclude the chapter with some of the insights that can make unbundling a more successful strategy.

Bundles do make buying decisions easier than à la carte offerings because buyers need to weigh fewer options than they would if they need to mix-and-match their own solution from scratch. Bundles are especially effective when they take advantage of preference reversals. Imagine a portfolio of two services, interior cleaning and exterior cleaning. The customer Acme Parts values the interior cleaning at $8,000 per month and the exterior cleaning at only $3,000 per month, while the customer Best Parts is basically the opposite. They value the interior cleaning at $3,500 per month and the exterior cleaning at $9,000 per month. In such a situation, it is impossible to set à la carte prices in a way that would generate more revenue – and more volume – than a pure bundle would generate. Figure 17.1 shows why.

The power of bundling holds even when the bundles are more complex and diverse than the straightforward example shown in Figure 17.1. But as you might imagine, when you have several potential products or services to include in a bundle, which ones you choose – and how many – will make a significant difference in how customers respond psychologically. We offer two caveats if you plan to bundle or unbundle products and services.

Customers' maximum willingness to pay

	Customer A (Acme Parts)	Customer B (Best Parts)
Interior cleaning	$8,000/mo	$3,500/mo
Exterior cleaning	$3,000/mo	$9,000/mo

Customers' maximum willingness to pay

À la carte (no bundling): Best case is to charge $8,000 or interior and $9,000 for exterior. You would sell one unit of each service and generate $17,000 in revenue

Pure bundle: Best case is to offer a combined package at $11,000, which means you sell two units of each and generate $22,000 in revenue each month

But any pure bundle price between $8,501 and $11,000 would outperform à la carte

Figure 17.1 Pure bundling outperforms à la carte pricing or mixed bundling when customer preferences vary widely

'Less is better': On a purely objective basis, finishing second is better than finishing third. It would therefore make sense that someone who finishes second should be happier with their performance than someone who finished third. But one study of Olympic medal winners showed the opposite effect: bronze medal winners tended to be happier with their medal than silver medal winners.[1] In essence, they were happier with less.

Likewise, it would make sense for someone to pay more for an eight-ounce serving of ice cream than a seven-ounce serving of exactly the same ice cream. But that is not true when the seven-ounce serving is crammed into a small container, while the eight-ounce serving comes in a ten-ounce cup that clearly leaves empty space at the top. The respondents in that study were willing to pay more for less.[2]

To understand why people make these clearly counterintuitive 'less is more' decisions, think back to our discussions of relativity in Part I. It is hard for people to make judgments unless they have a reference point or a pre-calibrated scale. One reason for this is the evaluability hypothesis, which states that when we evaluate something in isolation, our evaluations are often influenced by how easy attributes are to evaluate rather than how important the attributes are. Whenever we cannot make a direct relative judgment, our attention falls either on things we can easily observe and process, or on what we *aren't* getting in the deal rather than what we are getting. The athletes who won bronze are happy, because people who finish fourth at the Olympic Games do not get medals. But the athletes who won silver are disappointed, because someone else won gold.[3] Similarly, the customer at the ice cream shop feels rewarded when she sees seven ounces overflowing in a small cup, but feels cheated when the ten-ounce cup is not filled, even when the latter container has roughly 15% more ice cream than the former.[4]

Descriptive language is sufficient to alter someone's perception toward a lesser option, in the absence of visual or other sensory cues. Imagine that you are trying to select the final runner to represent your firm in a team 5k run to benefit a local charity.

'Well, we had a practice run yesterday', one of your colleagues says. 'Kerry finished second, but Kris came in next to last.' Based solely on that information, you would probably lean toward choosing Kerry to complete your team. What your colleague neglected to tell you, however, is that Kerry and Kris were the only two competitors in that practice run yesterday. Kerry finished second and last. Kris finished first, but technically speaking, also finished next to last.[5]

The lesson for bundling is that buyers will be influenced by the relative value of the individual components of a bundle. An additional product or service that exceeds expectations or seems disproportionately good will enhance a bundle, while an item that falls short of expectations will detract from the bundle's total value, even if that item is worth more in absolute terms.

University of Chicago behavioural science professor Christopher Hsee conducted an experiment that drives home that point. Respondents placed a higher value on a complete 24-piece set of dinnerware than they did on a collection of 31 pieces of dinnerware – including the original complete set, plus a few other pieces and some broken ones. The self-contained yet smaller set was more appealing than the larger set that included additional useful items and some inferior or unusable ones.[6]

Don't bundle very expensive things with cheap things: One additional lesson from those studies is that a seller should not bundle expensive items with very cheap items. The ghost of *homo economicus* would consider that statement to be illogical, because even cheap things add incremental value. How can adding value to a package – even a small amount – reduce the total value of the package?

Let's say you have a choice between buying a home gym and buying a gym membership. Wouldn't the home gym be more attractive if it came with a fitness DVD? Northwestern's Alexander Chernev and Pepperdine University's Aaron Brough tested that idea in five separate experiments and revealed that 'combining expensive and inexpensive items can lead to subtractive rather than additive judgments, such that consumers are willing to pay less for the combination than for the expensive item alone.'[7] In the case of the home gym and the gym membership, for example, the number of respondents who chose the home gym fell by 31% when the home gym came with the fitness DVD.[8] This occurs because people bucket the components of the bundle into broad qualitative categories – expensive, inexpensive, cheap – and then come up with an unweighted average of those categories. In the example of the gym, the equipment (expensive) and the DVD (cheap) average out to a net relative valuation that is less than the gym membership.

The ultimate test of a bundle is that the combination of products and services offers an advantage to both your customer and you. Just because you can theoretically group a few products together does not mean that the resulting combination will pass that test. The caveat here is that bundles are neither dumping grounds nor escape hatches for products you struggle to sell.

Bundling done well makes it easier for buyers to decide. It also enhances the differentiation of your offerings, by reducing the buyer's ability to make direct comparisons with competitive offerings and base their decisions solely on price. Bundling also creates opportunities to upsell. On the financial side, you should be aware that bundling can reduce your overall margin percentage, even though it can substantially increase your profits in absolute terms. The higher your fixed costs are, however, the less dramatic the margin percentage impact will seem.

Unbundling: The 'core' and 'cost' questions

It is tempting to think of bundling and unbundling as two sides of the same coin or two opposing directions along the same spectrum. But this is only partially true. The determining factors in a decision to unbundle a product or service are whether the offering in question is a core or non-core part of your business, and how volatile the costs of the product or service are.

We will start with the question of core versus non-core. In general, that is a fundamental strategic question far beyond the scope of this book. For the purposes of influencing buying decisions – and for unbundling in particular – there is a straightforward and practical way to distinguish between core and non-core. The latter encompasses those products and services that you procure and consume yourself but add no proprietary value. Mundane examples include packaging, shipping, storage, and third-party services such as legal support. With such clarity, we see no issue with price unbundling, which means that it often makes sense to charge separately and appropriately for shipping, out-of-pocket costs for a service call, or off-the-shelf materials.

Unbundling also helps a company cope with wide variations in cost to serve. These costs can be out-of-pocket costs, such as third-party costs to ship to remote or unplanned destinations, or inconvenience costs, such as when a client orders less than a truckload, orders outside pre-determined periods, orders containing custom sizes, or otherwise causes an unanticipated disruption to your operations. Ideally, you shouldn't be incurring costs unless those costs help you generate revenue and earn an appropriate margin. When a customer's behaviour causes you to incur extra costs, you can offset that burden by connecting those unexpected or above-and-beyond expenses to an additional service fee.

Unbundling also makes sense when you have features that are truly optional. You are under no obligation to offer all-inclusive packages to all customers, when it is more convenient and more practical to let customers decide what extras they need. Similarly, unbundling is an effective way to test the viability of new add-on services or enter new markets. In these situations, having more levers can help you gain greater trial and access than you would if you rolled all the features – new and old – into one offering with one price.

Finally, unbundling can be advantageous if customers pay particular attention to how much one aspect of your offering costs, but less attention to others. The rule of thumb is that you should design an offering in such a way that you are more competitive on the features that are at the customer's 'eye level' but can afford to charge higher prices on the features that the customer seems to care less about or devote less time to scrutinizing.

Despite this, unbundling also carries risks, especially when customers try to force their suppliers to unbundle an offering against their own interests. This 'divide-and-conquer' approach is a manifestation of the Digital Age, which has made transparency a fact of life. But sellers need to view buyers' pressure for transparency as a Trojan Horse. It is one thing to share information openly in the interest of serving customers and creating value for them. But it is another thing entirely for a supplier to reveal so much information that the buyers can abuse the transparency and come up with discrete, standardized offers that machines are able to process individually. Differentiation is the source of your advantages and your profits. Market standardization is the enemy of differentiation, which means that market standardization can be the enemy of profit. Don't let price become the sole difference between you and your competitors.

When the answer to 'bundle or unbundle?' is 'both'

Imagine that you work for a facilities management company that specializes in professional cleaning services for large buildings. At the moment, your projects are all based on the simplest of price calculations: $200 for a standard office of 2,000 square feet, all inclusive, no matter who the customer is.

But you have noticed that the disadvantages of a one-size-fits-all price often outweigh its extreme simplicity. Some office managers can be very creative when it comes to finding reasons to ask for a lower price, either because their office space is sparsely furnished or because they feel the cleaning requirements are not very demanding. Others see the price and make long lists of demands on your cleaning crews, so that they feel like they're getting the most for their money.

The term 'all inclusive' gives the impression that you are offering a bundle, but in the spirit of what we described above, such an all-inclusive offering is not a bundle. It does not make the customer's buying decision easier. It makes neither your operations nor your customers' more efficient. It makes the price the only differentiator in your value proposition. It leaves you no opportunities to upsell or use other techniques to influence a buyer's decision.

At the same time, your costs alone make this all-inclusive offering a prime candidate for unbundling. Suburban locations can be difficult to reach, not only because of the distance but because of rush-hour traffic. Customer demands may require you to use specialty chemicals or equipment to complete a job professionally, and these added costs can devour your margins in a hurry.

Figure 17.2 shows a before-and-after concept for how a cleaning service could take advantage of bundling *and* unbundling simultaneously in order to make itself more attractive, create revenue opportunities, and make it

OLD OFFERING

PROFESSINAL CLEANING

200^{00}

all inclusive
for a standard
2,000 sq ft office

NEW OFFERING

★
LEAN
Take care of the basics

- Crew of 2 for 2 hours
- Fixed price of $80
- Pre-agreed list of services
- City limits only
- Customer provides cleaning material in pre-agreed quantity/quality
- **Regular schedule**

80^{00}

fixed price

★★
STANDARD
Get the job done

- $25/h per crew member
- Size of crew depends on square footage and list of services outlined in the RFP
- Includes travel time and cost for crew up to 5
- Includes our own professional brand cleaning product
- **Flexible schedule**
  As per availability of staff

25^{00}/hr

★★★
FLEX
No worry

- $40/hr per crew member, billed monthly
- Size of crew depends on square footage and list of services outlined in the RFP
- Includes travel time and cost for all crew.
- Includes our own professional brand cleaning product
- **Late evening shifts after 8 pm.**
  Night shifts available upon request

40^{00}/hr

Plus *à la carte* menu of selected services

(e.g., specialized bags and bins, carpet deep cleaning, regular window cleaning)

Figure 17.2   A facilities management firm makes its offers more appealing and more differentiated through bundling and unbundling of its 'all inclusive' offer

easier for customers to choose an option that works for them without tedious negotiations that start from scratch.

The original motivation behind the old offering was simplicity and clarity. The company chose a nice round number for the price ($200), which seemed like a good average price for professional cleaning. The company also felt that it had established an anchor that could guide its negotiations. But the visible and invisible costs of using that simple approach were very high. First, the magic of differentiation lies in the distribution of customers, not their average. The appropriate price for a small suburban business with modest cleaning needs and the appropriate price for a high-profile downtown law firm might average out to $200, but the true costs of those jobs – and the quality expectations of the customers – could hardly be more different.

The bundles in the new approach allow customers to self-select their desired level of service by picking the offering they feel most comfortable with. The terms of each offering help ensure that costs will not explode and quality will not suffer if customers are demanding. Even if customers try to negotiate, the starting basis is much more reasonable.

Chapter 18

Decoys and the Power of 3

C ustomer tips make up a significant source of income for people in most service industries, especially in the United States. For taxi drivers in New York City, passengers would typically add around 10% to the fare when they handed the driver a handful of money after their rides.

But a new dynamic emerged in 2007 when New York City cab companies installed credit-card readers. By January 2012, around 55% of gross taxicab revenue came from credit-card transactions, up from around one-third in 2009 when the readers became standard.[1] Total revenue also increased significantly. One reason for this success is that using a credit card reduces the pain of paying.[2] When someone knows they can pay with a simple swipe of a credit card rather than search for cash or withdraw some from an ATM, they are more inclined to pay and potentially also to spend more.

Another dynamic, however, had even more powerful implications for New York's taxicab system and, more broadly speaking, for how a company can influence buying decisions. Instead of leaving passengers on their own to calculate a tip, the credit card display offers three specific amounts. These amounts were expressed in absolute dollars for shorter rides and in percentage terms – usually 15%, 20%, and 25% – for longer rides.

So, let's take a quiz. Prior to the addition of card readers, New York City taxi drivers received an average tip of around 10% per ride. Once riders had prompts to help with their decisions of tips, what did the average tip increase to?

a. It didn't increase at all,
b. it increased to 15%,
c. it increased to 18%, or
d. it increased to more than 20%.

Before we get to the answer, we'll look at the underlying concept, a universal phenomenon which is generally referred to as the Power of 3. Humans have a hard time finding and using a scale to calibrate quality. When faced with multiple options, they tend to gravitate to the 'golden' or 'magic' middle. As Itamar Simonson and Amos Tversky pointed out in their seminal paper on the topic, these decisions have less to do with the actual merits of the middle offer, and more to do with that they call extremeness aversion. The decisions that consumers make are 'often influenced by the context, defined by the set of alternatives under consideration'. They wrote, '[t]he attractiveness of an option is enhanced if it is an intermediate option in the choice set and is diminished if it is an extreme option.'[3]

There are several factors that determine how strong this effect is. The less frequently someone purchases a product – let's say a snow shovel – the more they may view the middle product and middle price as solutions that simplify their decision making and reduce their research costs. How the customer sees the information spatially also makes a difference. Building on the assumption that people prefer the middle option in a set,

Taiwanese researchers Chung-Chau Chang and Hsin-Hsien Liu revealed that 'an information format compatible with their characteristics makes the middle option more salient and attractive. In detail, the two researchers assert that the middle option becomes more attractive when presented in the middle position and more attractive when the buyer sees all the options together rather than separately.'[4] A subsequent study, which includes prices with the options, confirmed that the selection of the middle option is strongly influenced by its spatial presentation and not extremeness aversion or its related concept, the compromise effect, which states that people gravitate to a middle option when it seems to be a well-proportioned balance between two extremes.[5]

The tips in the New York City taxicab offer a massive and ongoing test of whether the Power of 3 not only holds true, but also whether its effects endure. So what is the answer to our quiz? It is 18%, which is roughly a doubling of the tips and a very good approximation of the middle option presented to customers.[6,7]

The practical implication of these studies is that if you have something you want a customer to choose, you do not give them your single best offer, nor do you focus on one alternative. Remember that the advanced version of the Invisible Game is about influencing decisions, not defining a choice. You offer the customer three alternatives in order to steer their eyes and their preference toward the option you have placed in the middle. To sum up the message in Figure 18.1, if you want people to buy more chicken and rice, you don't offer them better chicken and rice. You offer them sirloin steak.

The effectiveness of this approach is not limited to day-to-day consumers. It affects everyone, and it works best in complex sales situations in which the buyer can easily get overwhelmed or faces artificial pressures such as time. The presentation of three options simplifies their decision making.

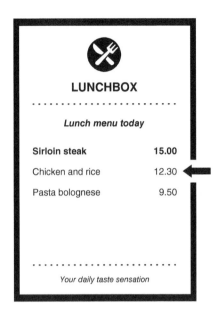

Figure 18.1 How the addition of a third, higher-priced option to a menu board increases the attraction of the middle option, which is no longer the most expensive one

The power of decoys

Imagine that you need an analyst with the skills to coordinate, crunch, and interpret a large number of complex datasets and spreadsheets. Your job advertisement attracts a lot of attention online, and your HR assistant helps you narrow down the candidates to two: Skyler, a recent MBA graduate from a prestigious business school in the eastern United States, and Taylor, a post-doctoral physicist from a highly respected Midwestern university. You have no clear choice based on their different backgrounds and personal pros and cons. Skyler had considerable work experience prior to business school, while Taylor wants to make the leap from academia to industry. You connect with each of them on a personal level, and you have full confidence that each would do excellent work and enrich your team.

The one remaining criterion that could separate them is salary expectations, but even that doesn't help as much as you expected. Skyler expects $130,000 and Taylor is asking for around $140,000 per year. That is a slight edge in Skyler's favour. Nonetheless, you still agonize over the decision and ask the two candidates to wait a little longer.

That's when your assistant brings you another candidate whose application came late in the process, after the first round of filtering. This new candidate, Jordan, just completed a PhD in physics at a decent university in midwestern United States. Jordan impresses you so much during the interview process that you now have three candidates who appear equally strong. As you conclude your own final interview with Jordan, you pose the question that will hopefully offer some guidance on whom to select.

'What are your salary expectations, Jordan?'

'Well, let me first say that I love atmosphere here, and I hope I'll get the opportunity to work here', Jordan says. Then the hammer falls. Citing the fresh doctorate in physics and a wide range of proven quantitative skills, Jordan calmly says that 'I can't settle for a job offer below $300,000.'

You let that number sink in, then smile and nod a few times.

'Thanks, Jordan, we'll be in touch very shortly. My assistant will walk you out.'

Your assistant returns a few minutes later, leans in the doorway, and looks you straight in the eye: 'So . . .?'

The question draws out the same smile you had after your interview with Jordan. Then you reveal the decision.

'I'm making a phone call this afternoon,' you say. 'Taylor gets the job. Let's get the paperwork ready.'

It turns out that Jordan facilitated the decision without ever standing a chance of landing the job. The salary expectation shifted your perception of the value of a doctorate in physics, relative to another graduate degree such as an MBA. Jordan unwittingly became what scientists refer to as a decoy. When two options seem equal, the introduction of a third option can allow someone distinguish between the two otherwise equal options and make a decision.

Decoys can affect choices in several ways. The irony of decoys is that you can strengthen your portfolio – and boost your sales – by including a product nobody wants to buy. Let's look at an example from a complex portfolio. GrindKlemp, a manufacturer of industrial packaging machines, had included four options in its portfolio for years. The four core machines – the A, B, C, D series models – addressed different market segments and helped them carve out a leadership position in terms of both market share and technology.[8] The machines had two main features: format and parts per minute. The format refers to whether the machine packs powder, gel, or both as sealed plastic capsules. Gel was the newer technology, but both formats were in demand in the market. Parts per minute refers to the number of individual items finished per minute. Table 18.1 below shows the standard prices and the specifications, ranging from the high-end D model down to the best-selling, mid-range C model to the basic A model.

When the venture capital arm of Chicago Entrepreneurs, Inc. (CEI) bought GrindKlemp, it looked for ways to reduce the size of the portfolio

Table 18.1 The specifications and list prices for GrindKlemp's portfolio of industrial packaging machines

Model	Format	Parts per minute	Price in US$ (millions)
D	Gel and powder	100	11.5
C	Gel and powder	97	6.0
B	Gel only	95	5.2
A	Powder only	80	3.0

from five models to four or even three. The B model looked like the prime target. It had a feature profile that didn't fit its price point very well, and it accounted for only about 3% of the company's sales. That sounded like an open-and-shut case. It was hard to argue against the B model's downward sales trend and its cost burden, never mind the distraction of building marketing and training programmes around five models instead of four.

'That could possibly be the worst move you could make', someone said at the meeting where the new owners proposed killing off the B model. The person was a regional sales rep that Chicago Entrepreneurs had kept in her role after the acquisition.

'Would you mind telling me why?' said the CEI team leader.

The sales rep proceeded to explain the history of the B model. GrindKlemp had considered killing it off two years earlier, but decided instead to test the portfolio in a couple of markets to see what the effect would be.

'One of those markets was mine', the rep said. 'When we took the B model out, we noticed that people gravitated toward the cheaper A model and away from the C, our best-selling unit. The B turned out to be a very effective decoy. We kept it in the portfolio because it makes the C look like a much better deal. We also did the maths and saw that the revenue gained from selling more C models more than offsets the cost of manufacturing and retaining the B.'

Joel Huber, John Payne, and Christopher Puto of Duke University first documented these kinds of decoy effects, which occur when an item in a set is 'asymmetrically dominated by one item in the set but not by another'.[9] In one of their studies, participants needed to choose between taking their date to a five-star restaurant which was a 25-minute drive away or to a three-star restaurant which was 5 minutes away. When the scientists introduced a third option – a five-star restaurant that was 35 minutes away – the study participants on average tended to favour the five-star restaurant located 25-minute drive away.

This is analogous to what GrindKlemp experienced. Practically speaking, the strategic role of the B model in the portfolio was not for customers to buy it. Instead, B's primary role is to make the C model stand out even more than it would objectively. As the researchers from Duke University wrote: 'Adding such an alternative to a choice set can increase the probability of choosing the item that dominates it. This result points to the inadequacy of many current choice models and suggests product line strategies that might not otherwise be intuitively plausible.'[10]

The Power of 3 and the decoy are complementary ideas, not contradictory ones. If the relationship between the three options is balanced or symmetrical, people naturally gravitate to the 'golden middle'. On the other hand, if the relationship between the three options is unbalanced or asymmetrical, people tend to prefer the option enhanced most by the asymmetry. It has been 40 years since the original fascinating study by the Duke researchers, but their findings remain an undiscovered gold mine whose effects have been underestimated or underappreciated, especially in B2B portfolios. Most key account executives and salespeople are unaware that many purchasers struggle with all the decisions they must make, and that decoys can make it easier for them to decide.

Very efficient levers for choice architectures with decoys are loss aversion, short-term benefits, and the value of zero. It remains up to you to decide precisely how you want you tap the Power of 3 and decoys to nudge your customers consistently and effectively to purchase the product you want them to buy. These techniques will not work every time, but in the long run, they skew the odds significantly in your favour.

Chapter 19

The Power of the Next Small Thing

Coming up with decoys or finding ways to use the power of now to your advantage, for example, may be sexy and creative challenges that people want to be part of. But there are also many small ways to influence the balance of power and change perceptions. These tasks may not come to mind immediately as powerful tactics, but they can help you set and reset frames, now and in the future. We highlight three of them in this chapter.

Restrict the other negotiating party's options

A party's personal power is diminished when something constrains their options or their flexibility. An example of a buyer imposing a power-limiting constraint is to set a deadline. By saying 'we need a deal by the end of the week', a buyer instantly leaves the seller with fewer degrees of freedom. Why does restricting options or imposing constraints diminish personal power? The reason is that it creates additional hurdles for the other party to overcome.

Overcoming a hurdle has a depletive effect. You only have so much capacity to deal with hurdles properly. The better way to succeed in a challenging situation is not to overcome hurdles, but to *eliminate* hurdles and not have them to begin with. Your best opportunity lies in exerting as much control as possible over the environment or frame. The more options you have, the better your chances are to eliminate variables and manage your environment. This is analogous to why we reframed the question of discounting in Part II to make it easier to say 'no' rather than harder to say 'yes'.

Surround yourself with strong allies

A party can enhance its power by cultivating relationships with other powerful parties that will lend their support if necessary. This obviously includes others in your own organization, but can also include business partners along the supply chain to strong outside references. Allies can even include members of the buyer's organization, such as the R&D team, senior executives, or even the buyer's customers.

The dimensions and density of your network matter. Having a strong network within your own organization increases your personal power, both inside your company and in the eyes of your customer. The company VoloMetrix examined the email exchanges of salespeople in a large organization and concluded that 'having a large and healthy network in your own organization' is a key success factor, because it enables salespeople to 'get the right people with the right expertise to the right place at the right time.'[1] It also helps salespeople convey a 'holistic understanding of what their entire company can offer to the buyer above and beyond the current transaction'. When selling the dream, a unified group effort enhances a buyer's perception of the supplier's competencies and capabilities more than any single salesperson could do on their own. Similar to a primate projecting its size in order to look more powerful and avoid a conflict, salespeople can increase their 'size' and power by coming across as the spearhead of a larger competent team rather than an individual actor.

Like all other recommendations in this book, there is hard scientific evidence for this. One of Kai's lines of research deals with the Cheerleader Effect and the Banker Effect. The former is well-established and characterizes the phenomenon that individuals in a group picture appear more attractive than when presented alone. The Banker Effect was discovered by Kai and his research colleagues Sonja Lehmann and Romy Eisenbichler. In a controlled online research investigation, the team flashed pictures of people – sometimes as part of a group and sometimes by themselves – to respondents who were asked to evaluate them on various criteria on scales from 0 to 100. They found out that the same individuals shown in a group are perceived to be not only more attractive, but also estimated to earn higher salaries and be slightly more intelligent. The Banker Effect, which indicates successful careers, is not a mere derivative of the Cheerleader Effect, as Lehmann demonstrated in an extensive multivariate analysis. The lesson for salespeople here is that presenting yourself as part of a group – whether in person or on a Zoom call – will enhance your perceived competence.

This is related to network density, which indicates how tightly knit those groups are. One of the more fascinating examples of network density occurs when a smaller company has an ally or friend in a high place within a much larger buyer's organization. This is another manifestation of the Invisible Game. The implicit threat – being able to go up the ladder and call in a favour if something goes wrong – confers power on the smaller party that it could never have on its own. We sometimes refer to this as scandalizing power, because no one on the buying team wants to attract that kind of negative personal attention. A System 1 response kicks in to prevent the buying team from undertaking any steps that could expose them and their careers to unnecessary risks. This is a subtle but important way to use personal power to limit another party's options. By taking certain responses off the table, the buying party is more likely to respond in a way that benefits the sellers. At the same time, the smaller selling party needs to be careful not to overplay its hand. Hollow threats and 'crying wolf' will diminish the power that the mere threat of scandalizing power exerts.

Controlling the mundane parts of the Visible Game

The first two sets of actions – restricting the other side's options and surrounding yourself with allies – have more of a strategic nature. They may make the third set of mostly tactical actions look mundane. These actions include setting the agenda, the timing and duration of a meeting, the seating plan within the meeting room, and who writes and distributes the minutes. Given the chance, many people will happily leave that work to the other party, because it's neither sexy nor apparently essential.

Yet that impression is deceptive. Each of these actions can play subtle and powerful roles in projecting power.

Let's look in detail at a few areas that can nudge the entire trajectory of the negotiation in your favour: the agenda and the minutes. These two aspects matter for two overarching reasons. First, any form of communication – but especially one that might travel beyond the people within the core teams on each side – is an opportunity to exercise personal power on something that seems dry, objective, and solely in the domain of paper power. Second, the frame and context – assuming that you own it – can become one of your strongest competitive advantages if you ensure that it lasts beyond the meeting.

The agenda can also determine people's perceptions during the meeting and also affect its outcome and its aftermath. To say that this is 'expectations management' is not sufficient, because precisely how you manage those expectations is what makes the difference between setting the frame or obfuscating it and potentially ceding the initiative to the other party.

It is tempting to view this exercise as low value, the kind of drudgery assignment a junior team member might do. It may also be tempting to let the buying team do that 'grunt work' so that you can focus on higher value activities. But we see setting a meeting agenda as a vital part of framing a negotiation.

You should also never underestimate the importance and power of writing the minutes. What happens after the meeting can prove to be even more important to enhancing personal power and establishing greater paper power. When your team writes the minutes, you decide what gets circulated outside the group, what information gets kept for future generations, and what information is suppressed or forgotten. This makes writing the minutes a high-value assignment that your team should try to do after every meeting.[2]

At a minimum, it provides you an opportunity to capture the events of the meeting in the best possible light for your team and company. In the best cases, it can alter the course of a negotiation. It also allows you to inform three audiences about what happened, and do it on your terms. The first audience is the attendees themselves, but that is not as obvious as you might think. You should write the minutes both for the current and future 'versions' of the attendees. The attendees may all read the minutes at a later date with a different mindset or different set of needs than they had at the meeting.

The second audience is those people who were not in attendance, including senior executives, managers from other functions such as product development, or even outside investors. The minutes allow them to experience and understand what happened at the meeting. The third audience is the relevant future reader who may not, currently, even be part of your or the buyer's organization. Teams often use meeting minutes to bring new colleagues up to speed, or as a template or benchmark for future negotiations.

The way you express what happened is also important. The minutes are not a dry record that merely expresses the agenda items in past tense with checkmarks. They represent the writer's selective memory and can serve as prompts, similar to the technique of prompts we described in Part II.

Specific words matter, as a study from the late 1970s showed.[3] In one landmark study into memory and recall, respondents were asked to view films of automobile accidents, followed by questions about the speed of the cars involved. The question 'About how fast were the cars going when they smashed into each other?' led to higher estimates of speed than the question 'About how fast were the cars going when they hit each other?' One week after seeing the film the respondents returned to answer another 10 questions, which included 'Did you see any broken glass?' The verb 'smashed' led not only to higher estimates of speed, but also to a higher number of positive responses about whether they had seen any glass. That last point is especially intriguing, because the videos the respondents watched did not show any broken glass.

The experiment demonstrates how leading questions and statements can influence responses. The study's authors also concluded that a complex occurrence leaves two kinds of information in a person's memory. The first is one's own perception of the original event. The second is external information supplied after the fact. Over time, information from both these sources may be integrated in such a way that people are unable to tell which specific detail came from which source.

Practically speaking, this means that writing the minutes is a subjective exercise, not an objective one. The choice of words puts the writer in a powerful position to not only decide what gets recorded, but also how it will be remembered. The minutes help you get people to see what you want them to see when they read between the lines. The meaning of the minutes is greater than the sum of their words.

What the minutes contain, and what they end with, will affect what readers retain. The minutes are a powerful and enduring communications tool. In a world in which people have increasingly short memories and can suffer from information overload, creating a memorable permanent record that people can access later can provide significant leverage to the team that writes the minutes.

CONCLUSION: HAS IT REALLY NEVER BEEN HARDER TO BE A SALESPERSON?

As we finished writing this book, we realized that once again we live in a time when salespeople feel they are facing an existential crisis. The world has changed and evolved beyond their recognition, but the expectations placed on them haven't. From the front lines of intercompany relationships, they are witnessing that businesses are rapidly transforming the way they source. This affects corporate salespeople as much as it affects independent professionals trying to build their businesses.

Procurement professionals are marginalizing salespeople by using online search capabilities and analytical tools to gather extensive information long before the first meeting, which now frequently takes place across a virtual negotiating table. These buyers are preying on the fears of salespeople, who suffer under the shadows of uncertainty, industry disruption, and rapidly advancing technology that threatens to displace them. Buyers turn those intimidating shadows into sharp tactical and psychological weapons that can make salespeople vulnerable and predictable.

The most dangerous part of these perceptions, however, is something that will surprise most salespeople, their leaders, and in many cases, their customers too.

They're exaggerated.

In *The Invisible Game* we have revealed that all sales negotiations involve two games of skill played by both parties simultaneously. We call them the Visible Game and the Invisible Game. Each has its own rules and its own success factors, but traditional sales trainings devote most of their time and energy to the tasks of the Visible Game. Until *The Invisible Game*, no one had curated the fascinating behavioural, psychological, and neuro-scientific insights of the past few decades, weighed them against extensive practical sales experience, and created a unified set of tactics, techniques, and skills that can help salespeople create new advantages and win deals on their terms. *The Invisible Game* shows salespeople how to enhance their situational awareness, defend against the strategies and tactics of buyers, and play offence in negotiations.

However, we feel we've done more than that. We have also shown sales-people how to carve out a vital role for themselves in their future, not suc-cumb to a diminished one. We've invited you to adopt a new mindset to instil the habits that will help you amass greater power and wield more options than you previously thought you could.

Making the ideas stick

Throughout the book we have captured some of most striking tips and tricks on stylized sticky notes. Along the way, you may have noted some additional insights or come up with your own personal ways to remember or reinforce some ideas. In feedback from countless workshops, salespeople have made one thing very clear: they internalize ideas and recommendations even more effectively when they write their own notes by hand and craft their own prompt materials. For that reason, we suggest that you make 'sticky' notes for your own ideas as reinforcement. If you would like to download the notes from the book, please visit www.wiley.com\go\theinvisiblegame.

EPILOGUE: SOME FINAL TAKEAWAYS FROM GABY AND KAI

Thank you for reading *The Invisible Game*. That means a lot to us. We were hoping to share our passion for the tremendous value that the Invisible Game adds to your side of the negotiation table. Each of us has some final thoughts and takeaways as we all get back to business. Kai will direct his at professors and trainers, while Gaby will follow with her takeaways for salespeople.

Kai's final takeaways

Dear Fellow Professors and Trainers,

For my classes and my workshops, I am always on the lookout for interesting new materials. To provide you with a compact way to introduce the Invisible Game and illustrate some of the differences between the Visible Game and the Invisible Game, you can use Table E.1. We intentionally left this piece of the puzzle until the end of the book, because we thought it was best appreciated after reading the entire book.

I am someone who learns most from examples and many of my students do so too. That's why I feel that the handful of examples in Table E.1 could give you an idea for a presentation slide or some leads to develop teaching materials. As with all our ideas – develop it further, adjust it to your industry of choice, and always feel free to send us an email with your best examples!

Table E.1 A few examples that illustrate the differences between the Visible Game and the Invisible Game

The Visible Game	The Invisible Game
Receiving an RFP for one of your products or services	Figuring out what anchors have been placed in that RFP
'We have a management meeting tomorrow and need your reply by tonight'	Recognizing time and timing as tactical moves to apply artificial stress
Sending out your proposal to your customer	Constructing an advantageous choice architecture for that proposal
Wearing a wristwatch	Using the wristwatch as a prompt to remind yourself of an intended action
Receiving a request for a discount within pre-defined parameters	Reply with no acknowledgment of the anchors embedded in the request
'We have a standard approach and process on how to manage a client.'	You have standards and processes for administration, but remain unpredictable for the other side when it is time for negotiation
'My customer always asks for new ideas but never follows up on them.'	Repeat the idea to the customer seven or eight times

Gaby's final takeaways

Dear Fellow Salespeople,

When preparing for a specific business situation, I tend to flip through my books repeatedly for quick advice and ideas. For those of you who like to do the same, here is my personal quick guide to *The Invisible Game*. It's organized by business topic and refers to the relevant chapter.

How to sustain healthy customer relationships

Customer strategies
- Evaluate your true position in the supplier segmentation. Think future! (Chapter 11).

- Risks of assumptions: Do you know, or do you *think* you know? (Chapter 2).
- The most valuable question may be: What should we stop doing? (Chapter 12).

New customers
- Programme first impressions actively to match your strategic intent (Chapter 3).
- Change needs to sound, look, and feel like change (Chapter 3).
- Always take the time to onboard new customer players (Chapter 4).

Joint meetings
- The tactical value of timeouts (Chapter 1).
- Keep presentations simple. Audiences love short messages (Chapter 3).
- New ideas need a lot of repetition to get heard (Chapter 3).
- Apply storytelling principles to create lasting memories (Chapter 12).
- Agendas and minutes shape the collective memory of success (Chapter 19).

How to improve your odds in a negotiation

Preparation
- Judgment calls versus choices (Chapter 1).
- Time for analysis: understand the frame you operate in (Chapter 3).
- Understand your customer's organizational focus (Chapter 12).
- Restrict the other party's options and surround yourself with allies (Chapter 19).

Choice architectures
- The psychology behind losses and gains (Chapter 15).
- The promise of getting something (small) now beats the promise of any long-term gain, even if the latter would be much larger (Chapter 16).

- Decisions shift toward the 'golden middle' option with three symmetrical alternatives (Chapter 18).
- Asymmetric choice architectures influence decisions toward the perceived 'better deal' (Chapter 18).

How to influence buying decisions

From your position

- Make the first move! The first number in a discussion will have a strong influence on the last number in that same discussion (Chapter 4).
- Develop the habit of 'anchoring' as part of your selling strategy (Chapter 4).
- Pitching: The difference between being the incumbent or the challenger (Chapter 12).
- 'Unbundling' helps suppliers with costs that have no proprietary value for them (Chapter 17).

From the buyer's position

- Was it a headshake or a handshake? (Chapter 1).
- Buyers need to hear the word 'no' (Chapter 9).
- When losing hurts more than winning excites (Chapter 8).
- Tactics: time, timing, uncertainty, fear, silence (Chapter 10).
- 'Bundling' can make customer decisions easier (Chapter 17).

How to manage pricing

New prices

- Prices translate into sensory experiences (Chapter 2).
- Prices and their relativity (Chapter 5).
- Prices are the outcome of stories (Chapter 5).
- Price thresholds may not be where you expect them (Chapter 12).
- Cost transparency (Chapter 14).

Re-pricing your portfolio
- Noticeable differences (Chapter 12).
- Price increases versus price adjustments (Chapter 13).
- The notion of fairness (Chapter 13).
- The calming routine of annual pricing discussions (Chapter 13).
- List prices as anchors (Chapter 14).

Requests for discounts and concessions
- Your dominant response should be NO! (Chapter 6).
- Countering anchor attempts (Chapter 10).
- Managing in the context of transactional relationships (Chapter 11).
- The psychology behind losses and gains (Chapter 15).
- Free should really be 'for free' (Chapter 16).

How self-management leads to better results and greater success
- Fight the comfort of stability. When business environments are in transition, the same old behaviours cannot solve new equations (Chapter 2).
- Whose deal have you won (success illusion)? (Chapter 2).
- Emotions that hinder success (Chapter 8).
- Push the boundaries to expand your comfort zone (Chapter 9).
- Our ingrained desire to be liked (Chapter 10).

Share your stories and questions

As you bring these insights back into your business world, you will encounter new experiences. We'd love to hear your stories about how you've applied the concepts, and what you achieved. To get in touch or share your thoughts or your personal stories on playing the Invisible Game, please send Gaby an email at invisiblegame@gabrielerehbock.com or contact Kai via invisiblegame@kai-markus-mueller.com.

ACKNOWLEDGEMENTS

It feels like some books write themselves. This is not one of them.

It was a true challenge for us to translate the trillions of ideas we had in our minds. Our goal was a book combining a solid scientific background, readability, and practical advice. That combination is what makes the collaboration between us so unique. And it was this combination that we urged to see reflected in *The Invisible Game*.

First and foremost, we thank Frank Luby for helping us make it happen. His brilliance and skills in providing professional structure to what started as an unsorted collection of concepts and insights made the book both readable and solid at the same time. Without Frank, the book would not exist. It is as simple as that. Wishing him and his wife Sue all the best, we are deeply grateful for several years of intense collaboration.

We also thank the team supporting Frank: Ezra Blocker, who helped proofread the final drafts and Tauni Howes, who transcribed our initial working sessions when we began writing the book.

We thank Black Fish Tank, especially, and Luna Margherita Cardilli and Ljudmilla Socci for stepping in at the last minute to design the sticky notes as an integral part of the book. Since our first encounter, we enjoyed your inspiring creativity and were amazed to see your magic unfold.

We thank Annie Knight, Corissa Hollenbeck, and Purvi Patel, as well as the entire Wiley publication, marketing, and sales teams. From the day we first met, their positive energy and excitement became contagious and helped us through some difficult finishing pains. We thank Premkumar Narayanan for help with proofreading. Special thanks go out to Danilo Zatta for the initial spark and introduction to Wiley.

We would like to thank Arnold van der Beek, Gaby's first-ever sales boss. As one of the best salespeople Gaby has ever met, he became a proof-of-principle reader and trusted consultant for our practical advice. Throughout her extended sales career, Gaby has worked with many teams on both sides of the negotiation table who somehow have all contributed to this book in one way or another. Unfortunately, they cannot be all named here. Representing many others, special thanks go out to Jeremy Celliers, Felix Frowein, Scott Violette and Elisabetta Soana, Gerardo Enriquez and Renaud Joly, Jean-Sebastien Degrange and Mark Haward, Cecile Seguy and Celine Maggia, Nils Mader, Clara Tri, and Javier Acosta.

We are grateful to Viktor Stebner, Tobias Hahn, Julia Kästle, Janine Rau, and Sara Bertsch for insightful comments and suggestions on previous versions of this manuscript. Also, Viktoria Frese gave us thoughtful feedback and helped us organize our reference database.

And we thank our families for their support and patience when we spent endless hours on video conferences with each other or with Frank.

Gaby: I thank my sister and my brother and their families so close to my heart for their love and encouragement, and in particular Peter, my husband and love of my life, for his inspiration, practical advice and humour. Joy and love are the key ingredients of happiness, and each morning I wake up to days full of both.

Kai: I thank my wife Katja for all her love as well as her acceptance of and patience with my crazy writing schedules – it is fabulous to have all that backing. Of course, I thank Lina and Karlotta for the daily dose of sunshine and happiness they bring to our lives. Finally, thanks to every one of the Müller and Holderle families for all the constant support.

ABOUT THE AUTHORS

Kai-Markus Mueller is Director of Pricing Research at the international consumer neuroscience agency Neurensics in Amsterdam. He is also Professor of Consumer Behavior at HFU Business School in Schwenningen, Germany. His core areas of expertise and research are the impact of psychology and neuroscience on pricing decisions and the perception of prices. Kai masterminded the development of NeuroPricing™, a research tool ultimately acquired by Neurensics that uses EEG brain scans to analyse a consumer's willingness to pay. Previously, he worked for several years as a start-up entrepreneur, as a pricing consultant with global management advisors Simon-Kucher & Partners, and as a neurophysiologist at the National Institute of Health in Bethesda, MD. He holds a PhD in neuroscience.

Gabriele Rehbock has over 30 years of experience in industrial sales, marketing, and management. As a top executive in the fragrance division of the Firmenich Group, one the leaders in the fragrance and flavour industry, she worked closely with a variety of customers – from multinationals to mid-size companies – in the United States, Europe, and Asia. The account teams she personally recruited and trained have earned numerous industry awards for outstanding performance. The very nature of this industry confronts salespeople with a major challenge: how to sell a product that the customer cannot see or touch, only smell. Her experiences gave her a nuanced understanding of the cultural differences that influence negotiations. As a consultant for B2B sales strategies, she now shares her expertise worldwide with clients in diverse industries.

NOTES

Introduction

1. This anecdote is based on several true stories, edited and combined for clarity.
2. Thaler, R. (1980). Toward a positive theory of consumer choice. *Journal of Economic Behavior and Organization 1*, 39–60.
3. See Thaler, R.H., Sunstein, C.R., and Balz, J.P. (2010). Choice architecture. *The Behavioral Foundations of Public Policy* April: n.p.
4. Müller, K.M. (2012). *NeuroPricing – wie Kunden über Preise denken*. Freiburg and Munich: Haufe-Lexware.
5. American Chemical Society International Historic Chemical Landmarks. (n.d.). *Discovery and Development of Penicillin*. ASC. Retrieved May 25, 2022, from https://www.acs.org/content/acs/en/education/whatischemistry/landmarks/flemingpenicillin.html (accessed 25 May 2022).
6. Britannica, T.E.E. (2021, December 25). Charles Goodyear. *Encyclopaedia Britannica*. https://www.britannica.com/biography/Charles-Goodyear (accessed 25 May 2022).
7. This anecdote is based on several true stories, edited and combined for clarity.
8. This is known as the Stroop Phenomenon. See a Stroop Table for further illustration: *Stroop Phenomenon*. (n.d.). [Table]. https://musingsofanaspie.files.wordpress.com/2014/11/stroop.jpg?w=672&h=244&crop=1 (accessed 4 August 2022).
9. Kahneman, D. (2011). *Thinking, Fast and Slow*. New York: Farrar, Straus and Giroux.

10. The Dutch neuroscience research agency Neurensics, which applies psychological studies and brain research to answer marketing questions, has since acquired the NeuroPricing™ suite.

11. Petty, R.E. and Cacioppo, J.T. (1986). The elaboration likelihood model of persuasion. In: *Communication and Persuasion,* 1–24. New York: Springer.

12. Haidt, J. (2006). *The Happiness Hypothesis: Finding Modern Truth in Ancient Wisdom*. New York: Basic Books.

13. Kahneman, D. (2011). *Thinking, Fast and Slow*. New York: Farrar, Straus and Giroux.

Part I: Building Your Situational Awareness

1. Sullivan, T. (2019, January 1). Bill Belichick sings praises of NFL referees. *247sports*. https://247sports.com/nfl/new-england-patriots/Article/Bill-Belichick-NFL-referees-127159556/ (accessed 25 May 2022).

2. Portugal break England hearts. (2004, June 24). *BBC Sport*. http://news.bbc.co.uk/sport2/hi/football/euro_2004/3830451.stm (accessed 25 May 2022).

3. One example of the never-ending scrutiny of history – at least in soccer – is the 1966 World Cup final, which ended in controversy when Geoff Hurst scored a goal in extra time to put England ahead of West Germany, 3–2. The Germans contend that the ball never crossed the end line. The English contend otherwise. England eventually won the match and the World Cup by a 4–2 score.

4. Henley, J. (2004, October 13). 'It was the right decision. Absolutely.' *The Guardian*. https://www.theguardian.com/football/2004/oct/13/newsstory.sport10 (accessed 25 May 2022).

5. Henley, J. (2004, October 13). 'It was the right decision. Absolutely.' *The Guardian*. https://www.theguardian.com/football/2004/oct/13/newsstory.sport10 (accessed 25 May 2022).

6. Meier, U. and Mendlewits, D. (2010). *Du Bist Die Entscheidung: Schnell Und Entschlossen Handeln*. Frankfurt am Main: Fischer Taschenbuch.

Chapter 1: The Forces Behind the Invisible Game

1. Andersen, J.A. (2000). Intuition in managers – are intuitive managers more effective? *Journal of Managerial Psychology* 15 (1): 46–67.

2. Kahneman, Daniel. *Thinking, Fast and Slow* (p. 13). London: Penguin. Kindle Edition.
3. MLB Tonight and Mark Derosa (2020, February 22). 30 for 30: Adam Eaton breaks down tee hitting, [Video]. YouTube. https://www.youtube.com/watch?v=itDo98iNdiw (accessed 4 August 2022).

Chapter 3: Controlling Illusions = Controlling the Deal

1. Hasher, L., Goldstein, D., and Toppino, T. (1977). Frequency and the conference of referential validity. *Journal of Verbal Learning and Verbal Behavior* 16 (1): 107–112.
2. Brashier, N.M. and Marsh, E.J. (2020). Judging truth. *Annual Review of Psychology* 71: 499–515.
3. Tversky, A. and Kahneman, D. (1973). Availability: a heuristic for judging frequency and probability. *Cognitive Psychology* 5 (2): 207–232.
4. The most inspiring Coco Chanel quotes to live by. (2018, August 17). *Vogue Australia*. https://www.vogue.com.au/fashion/news/the-most-inspiring-coco-chanel-quotes-to-live-by/image-gallery/b1cb17be7e20734d0b255fb-d5a478ed4 (accessed 25 May 2022).
5. Fisher, L. A. (2020, February 19). Karl Lagerfeld's wittiest, most iconic, and most outrageous quotes of all time. *Harper's Bazaar*. https://www.harpersbazaar.com/fashion/designers/a26405187/karl-lagerfeld-quotes/ (accessed 25 May 2022).
6. For an additional perspective, see Watkins, M. (2013). *The First 90 Days: Proven Strategies for Getting Up to Speed Faster and Smarter*. Boston, MA: Harvard Business Review Press.
7. Nickerson, R.S. (1998). Confirmation bias: a ubiquitous phenomenon in many guises. *Review of General Psychology* 2 (2): 175–220.
8. A widely circulated story of unknown origin.
9. Gilovich, T., Keltner, D., Chen, S. et al. (2018). *Social Psychology*. London: W. W. Norton and Company.
10 You can watch the video here: Simons, D.S. (2010, April 28). *The Monkey Business Illusion* [Video]. YouTube. https://www.youtube.com/watch?v=IGQmdoK_ZfY (accessed 4 August 2022).

Chapter 4: Relativity and Anchoring: The Illusion of Numbers

1. This experiment is described in detail here: Ariely, D. (2008). *Predictably Irrational: The Hidden Forces that Shape Our Decisions*. New York: HarperCollins, pp. 26–31.
2. Do Hoang, V.K. and Tham, S. (2018, September 21). *Using Behavioural Insights to Increase Charitable Donations*. Civil Service College Singapore. https://www.csc.gov.sg/articles/using-behavioural-insights-to-increase-charitable-donations (accessed 25 May 2022).
3. *Rules for Sons*. (2018, March 12). The Good Men Project. https://goodmen-project.com/featured-content/rules-sons-gentleman-lbkr/ (accessed 25 May 2022).
4. Galinsky, A.D. (2004, August 9). *When to Make the First Offer in Negotiations*. Harvard Business School. https://hbswk.hbs.edu/archive/when-to-make-the-first-offer-in-negotiations (accessed 25 May 2022).
5. Gunia, B., Swaab, R., Savanthan, N. et al. (2013). The remarkable robustness of the first-offer effect: across culture, power, and issues. *Personality and Social Psychology Bulletin* 39, 12. https://www.researchgate.net/publica-tion/255959274_The_Remarkable_Robustness_of_the_First-Offer_Effect_Across_Culture_Power_and_Issues (accessed 25 May 2022).

Part II: Playing Defence and the Power of 'No'

1. For more information, please see the lab's website https://www.rnl.caltech.edu,
2. Plassmann, H., O'Doherty, J., Shiv, B. et al. (2008). Marketing actions can modulate neural representations of experienced pleasantness. *Proceedings of the National Academy of Sciences* 105 (3): 1050–1054.
3. Rao, A.R. and Monroe, K.B. (1989). The effect of price, brand name, and store name on buyers' perceptions of product quality: an integrative review. *Journal of Marketing Research* 26 (3): 351–357.
4. Knutson, B., Rick, S., Wimmer, G.E. et al. (2007). Neural predictors of purchases. *Neuron* 53 (1): 147–156.
5. Thadeusz, F. (2013, October 10). *Using Brainwaves to Test Prices*. Spiegel International. Retrieved May 27, 2022, from https://www.spiegel.de/

international/zeitgeist/scientist-uses-brainwaves-to-test-ideal-prices-for-products-a-926807.html (accessed 25 May 2022).

6. Parikh, H., Baldo, D., and Müller, K.-M. (2017). Pricing. In: *Consumer Neuroscience* (ed. M. Cerf and M. Garcia-Garcia), 241–254. Cambridge, MA: MIT Press.

Chapter 5: Price = Maths + Story

1. Akerlof, G. and Shiller, R.J. (2009). *Animal Spirits: How Human Psychology Drives the Economy, and Why It Matters for Global Capitalism*. Princeton, NJ: Princeton University Press.

2. French, D. (2017, October 14). Mises killed homo economicus long before Thaler. *Mises*. https://mises.org/wire/mises-killed-homo-economicus-long-thaler (accessed 27 May 2022).

3. Thompson, D. (2017, October 9). Richard Thaler wins the Nobel in economics for killing *homo economicus*. *The Atlantic*. https://www.theatlantic.com/business/archive/2017/10/richard-thaler-nobel-economics/542400/ (accessed 27 May 2022).

4. Smith, S.V. and Garcia, C. (2019, June 14). *Animal Spirits*. NPR. https://www.npr.org/2019/06/14/732876763/animal-spirits?t=1653657652619 (accessed 27 May 2022).

5. Glasswhere is a fictitious name, and the circumstances have been altered to anonymize this example.

6. Hayward, T. (2009, March 5). A successful brand - but of what? *The Guardian*. https://www.theguardian.com/lifeandstyle/wordofmouth/2009/mar/05/gordon-ramsay-restaurant-brand (accessed 27 May 2022).

Chapter 6: Psyched Up or Psyched Out?

1. Posts from the radio station saved here as screenshots: www.kai-markus-mueller.com/references-invisible-game (accessed 22 July 2022).

2. Zajonc, R.B., Heingartner, A., and Herman, E.M. (1969). Social enhancement and impairment of performance in the cockroach. *Journal of Personality and Social Psychology* 13 (2): 83–92.

3. Zajonc, R.B., Heingartner, A., and Herman, E M. (1969). Social enhancement and impairment of performance in the cockroach. *Journal of Personality and Social Psychology* 13 (2): 83–92.

Chapter 7: Paying the Price of 'Yes'

1. Wong, D. (2020, February 17). What science says about discounts, promotions and free offers. CM Commerce. https://cm-commerce.com/academy/what-science-says-about-discounts-promotions-and-free-offers/ (accessed 27 May 2022).
2. The gross margin of 20% may seem high for many B2B business. The detrimental effects of discounting, however, are even more extreme, if the company's margins were lower.
3. Marrs, J. and Kennedy, D. S. (2012, April 30). Is your staff sabotaging your pricing strategy? *Entrepreneur*. https://www.entrepreneur.com/article/223410 (accessed 27 May 2022).
4. 5. reasons why salespeople are quick to discount. (n.d.). *Pricing Brew Journal*. https://www.pricingbrew.com/insights/5-reasons-why-salespeople-are-quick-to-discount/ (accessed 27 May 2022).
5. Simester, D. and Zhang, J. (2014). Why do salespeople spend so much time lobbying for low prices?. *Marketing Science* 33 (6): 796–808.
6. Smith, T.J. (2016, July 3). How to stop discounting practices of salespeople from destroying your profits. *Wiglaf Journal*. https://wiglafjournal.com/how-to-stop-discounting-practices-of-salespeople-from-destroying-your-profits/ (accessed 27 May 2022).

Chapter 8: Overcoming the Fear of 'No'

1. Cambridge University Press. (n.d.). Price. *Cambridge Dictionary*. https://dictionary.cambridge.org/us/dictionary/english/price (accessed 30 May 2022).
2. Mustaghni, B., Lehrke, S., Archacki, R. et al. (2021, March 8). *Building Bionic Capabilities for B2B Marketing*. Boston Consulting Group. https://www.bcg.com/publications/2021/building-bionic-capabilities-to-improve-b2b-marketing (accessed 27 May 2022).
3. Roth, G. and Herbst, S. (2019). *Warum es so schwierig ist, sich und andere zu ändern: Persönlichkeit, Entscheidung und Verhalten*. Stuttgart: Klett-Cotta.
4. Kahneman developed the theory together with Amos Tversky, but Tversky had passed away before the awarding of the Nobel Prize. The prizes are not awarded posthumously.
5. The circumstances of this meeting have been simplified and disguised.

6. Geertz, C. (1973). *The Interpretation of Cultures*. New York: Basic Books, 259–260.
7. Geertz, C. (1973). *The Interpretation of Cultures*. New York: Basic Books, 117.

Chapter 9: Expand Your Comfort Zone

1. See for example: Fisher, Roger and Ury, William. (1991). *Getting to Yes: Negotiating Agreement without Giving In*. New York: Penguin.
2. Voss, P. (2017). *Dynamic brains and the changing rules of neuroplasticity: implications for learning and recovery*. *Frontiers*. Retrieved May 28, 2022, from https://www.frontiersin.org/articles/10.3389/fpsyg.2017.01657/full (accessed 28 May 2022).
3. Sapolsky, R.M. (2018). *Behave*. Kindle edition. London: Penguin Publishing Group, 136.
4. Bargh, J.A., Gollwitzer, P.M., Lee-Chai, A. et al. (2001). The automated will: nonconscious activation and pursuit of behavioral goals. *Journal of Personality and Social Psychology* 81 (6): 1014–1027.
5. Storch, M., Gaab, J., Küttel, Y. et al. (2007). Psychoneuroendocrine effects of resource-activating stress management training. *Health Psychology* 26 (4): 456–463.
6. Storch, M., Keller, F., Weber, J. et al. (2011). Psychoeducation in affect regulation for patients with eating disorders: a randomized controlled feasibility study. *American Journal of Psychotherapy* 65 (1): 81–93.
7. Liao, Y., Gao, G., and Peng, Y. (2019). The effect of goal setting in asthma self-management education: a systematic review. *International Journal of Nursing Sciences* 6 (3): 334–342.
8. Roney, C.J. and Lehman, D.R. (2008). Self-regulation in goal striving: individual differences and situational moderators of the goal-framing/performance link. *Journal of Applied Social Psychology* 38 (11): 2691–2709.
9. Matthews, G. (2007). *The Impact of Commitment, Accountability, and Written Goals on Goal Achievement*. Psychology: Faculty Presentations. 3. https://scholar.dominican.edu/psychology-faculty-conference-presentations/3 (accessed 5 August 2022).
10. Harkin, B., Webb, T.L., Chang, B.P.I. et al. (2016). Does monitoring goal progress promote goal attainment? A meta-analysis of the experimental evidence. *Psychological Bulletin*: 142 (2): 198–229.

11. Rogers, T. and Milkman, K.L. (2016). Reminders through association. *Psychological* Science 27 (7): 973–986.
12. Handy, T.C., Grafton, S.T., Shroff, N.M. et al. (2003). Graspable objects grab attention when the potential for action is recognized. *Nature Neuroscience* 6 (4): 421–427.
13. Storch, M. (2004). Resource activating self-management with the Zurich Resource Method. *European Psychotherapy* 5 (1): 27–64, 44.
14. In the original ZRM literature those permanent props are referred to as 'Chronic Primes'. The term 'priming' implies a pre-conscious mechanism. While we have a good empirical basis to believe that the props/primes work as intended, it is beyond the topic of this book to discuss whether those mechanisms are based on conscious, pre-conscious, or both kinds of processes.

Chapter 10: From the Buyer's Playbook: Time, Uncertainty, Fear, and Silence

1. *English Standard Version Bible* (2001). Luke 10: 29–37.
2. Belludi, N. (2015, June 16). *Lessons from the Princeton Seminary Experiment: People in a Rush are Less Likely to Help Others (and Themselves)*. Right Attitudes. https://www.rightattitudes.com/2015/06/16/people-in-a-rush-are-less-likely-to-help-themselves/ (accessed 27 May 2022).
3. The names and some situational details have been changed, but the story is based on a real event.
4. The perfect piece of toast: Scientists test 2,000 slices and find 216 seconds is the optimum time. (2011, July 22). The *Daily Mail*. Retrieved May 27, 2022, from https://www.dailymail.co.uk/sciencetech/article-2017338/The-perfect-piece-toast-Scientists-test-2-000-slices-216-seconds-optimum-time.html (accessed 27 May 2022).
5. Fredine, E. (2019, July 22). *What Stephen King Can Teach You About Writing Great Horror*. Writing Cooperative. https://writingcooperative.com/what-stephen-king-can-teach-you-about-writing-great-horror-67bcd9a9c56e (accessed 27 May 2022).
6. Both company names, as well as their industry, are fictitious to disguise the underlying real-life example.

Chapter 11: Personal versus Paper Power: Where's Your Leverage?

1. O'Conner, P.T. and Kellerman, S. (2018, November 14). *The Grammarphobia Blog: That's Why They Play the Game*. Grammarphobia. https://www.grammarphobia.com/blog/2018/11/thats-why-they-play-the-game.html (accessed 28 May 2022).
2. The ABC analysis first appeared in an article by General Electric's H. Ford Dickie. (1951, July). ABC inventory analysis shoots for dollars, not pennies. *Factory Management and Maintenance* 109: 92–94.
3. For more information, see https://www.juran.com/blog/a-guide-to-the-pareto-principle-80-20-rule-pareto-analysis/ (accessed 5 August 2022).

Chapter 12: What Buyers Think and How They Make Decisions

1. This story is based on an actual experience.
2. Thaler, R. (1980). Toward a positive theory of consumer choice. *Journal of Economic Behavior and Organization* 1 (1): 39–60.
3. Kahneman, D., Knetsch, J.L., and Thaler, R.H. (1991). Anomalies: the endowment effect, loss aversion, and status quo bias. *Journal of Economic Perspectives* 5 (1); 193–206.
4. Ericson, K.M.M. and Fuster, A. (2013). The Endowment Effect. NBER working paper series, Working paper 19384. Cambridge, MA 02138: National Bureau of Economic Research.
5. This anecdote is based on a true story, edited and simplified for clarity.
6. Arkes, H.R. and Blumer, C. (1985). The psychology of sunk cost. *Organizational Behavior and Human Decision Processes* 35 (1): 124–140.
7. Arkes, H.R. and Blumer, C. (1985). The psychology of sunk cost. *Organizational Behavior and Human Decision Processes* 35 (1): 124–140.
8. Arkes, H. R. and Blumer, C. (1985). The psychology of sunk cost. *Organizational Behavior and Human Decision Processes* 35 (1): 124–140.
9. Full disclosure: Kai is affiliated with Neurensics. He managed the conceptual and neuroscientific aspects of the respective study.

10. All numerical records in this paper have been modified from the original data in order to protect the client's confidentiality. However, the rationale of the project remains unaltered.

11. Herbes, C., Friege, C., Baldo, D. et al. (2015). Willingness to pay lip service? Applying a neuroscience-based method to WTP for green electricity. *Energy Policy*, 87: 562–572.

12. For additional information, see Nutter, F. (2010). *Encyclopedia of Research Design*. Los Angeles: SAGE Publications, 1613–1615.

13. *Weber's Law of Just Noticeable Differences*. (n.d.). USD Internet Sensation & Perception Laboratory. http://apps.usd.edu/coglab/WebersLaw.html (accessed 5 August 2022).

14. Müller, K.M. (2020, June 12). A discount of 3% on everything? Politicians should learn from pricing! LinkedIn. https://www.linkedin.com/pulse/discount-3-everything-politicians-should-learn-from-pricing-mueller/ (accessed 27 May 2022).

Chapter 13: What Is Your Re-pricing Strategy?

1. Mittal, V. (2019). A better way to price B2B offerings. AMA www.ama.org/marketing-news/a-better-way-to-price-b2b-offerings/ (accessed 22 July 2022).

2. Izaret, J.-M. (2022). Solving the paradox of fair prices. www.bcg.com/en-us/publications/2022/considering-pricing-variation-to-help-solve-the-paradox-of-fair-prices (accessed 22 July 2022).

3. Mittal, V. (2019). A better way to price B2B offerings. www.ama.org/marketing-news/a-better-way-to-price-b2b-offerings/ (accessed 22 July 2022).

4. Tabibnia, G. and Lieberman, M.D. (2007). Fairness and cooperation are rewarding: evidence from social cognitive neuroscience. *Annals of the New York Academy of Sciences* 1118 (1): 90–101.

5. Tabibnia, G., Satpute, A.B., and Lieberman, M.D. (2008). The sunny side of fairness: preference for fairness activates reward circuitry (and disregarding unfairness activates self-control circuitry). *Psychological Science* 19 (4): 339–347.

6. Thaler, R.H., Sunstein, C.R., and Balz, J.P. (2010, April). Choice architecture. *SSRN*. https://papers.ssrn.com/sol3/papers.cfm?abstract_id=1583509 (accessed 5 August 2022).

Chapter 15: Why Equal Things Aren't Always Equal

1. Kahneman, D. and Tversky, A. (1979). Prospect theory: an analysis of decision under risk. *Econometrica* 47 (2): 263–292.
2. Kahneman, D. and Tversky, A. (1979). Prospect theory: an analysis of decision under risk. *Econometrica* 47 (2): 263–292.
3. This 'boiling-frog phenomenon' is an urban legend, or more precisely another example of the illusory truth effect that we discussed in Part I. According to many experts, the phenomenon is not true.
4. Kahneman, D. and Tversky, A. (1979). Prospect theory: an analysis of decision under risk. *Econometrica* 47 (2): 263–292.

Chapter 16: The Power of Free and the Power of Now

1. Shampanier, K., Mazar, N., and Ariely, D. (2007). Zero as a special price: the true value of free products. *Marketing Science* 26 (6): 742–757.
2. Ariely, D., Gneezy, U., and Haruvy, E. (2018). Social norms and the price of zero. *Journal of Consumer Psychology* 28 (2): 180–191.
3. Camerer, C. (1999). Behavioral economics: reunifying psychology and economics. *Proceedings of the National Academy of Sciences* 96 (19): 10575–10577.

Chapter 17: To Bundle or Not to Bundle: Is that Really the Question?

1. Medvec, V.H., Madey, S.F., and Gilovich, T. (1995). When less is more: counterfactual thinking and satisfaction among Olympic medalists. *Journal of Personality and Social Psychology* 69 (4): 603.
2. Hsee, C.K. (1998). Less is better: when low-value options are valued more highly than high-value options. *Journal of Behavioral Decision Making* 11 (2): 107–121.
3. Medvec, V.H., Madey, S.F., and Gilovich, T. (1995). When less is more: counterfactual thinking and satisfaction among Olympic medalists. *Journal of Personality and Social Psychology* 69 (4): 603.

4. Hsee, C.K. (1998). Less is better: when low-value options are valued more highly than high-value options. *Journal of Behavioral Decision Making* 11 (2): 107–121.

5. This story is based on a tale from the Cold War era, when *Pravda* (the official newspaper of the Soviet Union) supposedly claimed that Soviet premier Nikita Khruschev finished second in a foot race, while the much younger and fitter US President John F. Kennedy came in next to last. The report conveniently omitted the fact that the two world leaders were the only ones competing in the race.

6. Hsee, C.K. (1998). Less is better: when low-value options are valued more highly than high-value options. *Journal of Behavioral Decision Making* 11 (2): 107–121.

7. Brough, A.R. and Chernev, A. (2011). When opposites detract: categorical reasoning and subtractive valuations of product combinations. *Journal of Consumer Research* 39 (2): 399–414.

8. Brough, A.R. and Chernev, A. (2019, May 11). When two products are less than one. Kellogg Insight. https://insight.kellogg.northwestern.edu/article/when_two_products_are_less_than_one (accessed 27 May 2022).

Chapter 18: Decoys and the Power of 3

1. Mann, T. (2012, February 27). More decide to charge a taxi ride. *The Wall Street Journal*. https://www.wsj.com/articles/SB1000142405297020452020 4577247850694349844 (accessed 28 May 2022).

2. Zellermayer, O. (1996). The pain of paying. PhD thesis. Carnegie Mellon University. https://www.google.com/search?q=the+pain+of+paying+Zellerma yer&source=lmns&bih=730&biw=1517&rlz=1C1CHBF_en-GBGB902GB902& hl=en&sa=X&ved=2ahUKEwjj3ee88K_5AhUHkRoKHbrND WsQ_AUoAHoECAEQAA.

3. Simonson, I. and Tversky, A. (1992). Choice in context: tradeoff contrast and extremeness aversion. *Journal of Marketing Research* 29 (3): 281–295.

4. Chang, C.-C. and Liu, H.-H. (2008). Information format-option characteristics compatibility and the compromise effect. *Psychology & Marketing* 25 (9): 881–900.

5. Ackermann, T. (2021, February). An investigation on the compromise effect: does familiarity drive preference for the spatial middle option? Bachelor thesis. Hochschule Furtwangen.

6. Grynbaum, M.M. (2009, November 7). New York's cabbies like credit cards? Go figure. *The New York Times*. https://www.nytimes.com/2009/11/08/nyregion/08taxi.html (accessed 28 May 2022).

7. Mann, T. (2012, February 27). More decide to charge a taxi ride. *The Wall Street Journal*. https://www.wsj.com/articles/SB10001424052970204520204577247850694349844 (accessed 28 May 2022).

8. This example is based on a true story, but the sector and data have been altered to ensure confidentiality.

9. Huber, J., Payne, J.W., and Puto, C. (1982). Adding asymmetrically dominated alternatives: violations of regularity and the similarity hypothesis. *Journal of Consumer Research* 9 (1): 90–98.

10. Huber, J., Payne, J.W., and Puto, C. (1982). Adding asymmetrically dominated alternatives: violations of regularity and the similarity hypothesis. *Journal of Consumer Research* 9 (1): 90–98.

Chapter 19: The Power of the Next Small Thing

1. Fuller, R. (2014, August 20). 3 behaviours that drive successful salespeople. *Harvard Business Review*. https://hbr.org/2014/08/3-behaviors-that-drive-successful-salespeople (accessed 28 May 2022).

2. Rehbock, G. (2022). Hello from the other side! *insights* 37: 10–11.

3. Loftus, E.F. and Palmer, J.C. (1974). Reconstruction of automobile destruction: an example of the interaction between language and memory. *Journal of Verbal Learning & Verbal Behavior* 13 (5): 585–589.

INDEX

wine and price level, brain
    response to 66–7

'yes'
    to discount 89
    as dominant response 85
    science behind 93–103
yes/no questions 25

Zajonc, Robert 76–7, 82
zero point 99
zero-risk bias 185
Zoom call 116
ZRM (Zuercher Ressourcen
    Modell, or Zurich Resource
    Model) approach 111,
    112, 113, 117